microprocessor background for management personnel

microprocessor background for management personnel

James Arlin Cooper

Sandia Laboratories
Albuquerque, New Mexico

PRENTICE-HALL, INC., *Englewood Cliffs, New Jersey*

Library of Congress Cataloging in Publication Data
COOPER, JAMES ARLIN.
   Microprocessor background for management personnel.
   Includes bibliographies and index.
   1. Microprocessors. I. Title.
QA76.5.C634   *001.64 '04*   80-16559
ISBN 0-13-580829-4

Editorial production supervision
  and interior design by Karen Winkler.
Cover design by George Alon Jaediker.
Manufacturing buyer: Joyce Levatino.

Printed in the United States of America

10 9 8 7 6 5 4 3 2 1

Prentice-Hall International, Inc., *London*
Prentice-Hall of Australia Pty. Limited, *Sydney*
Prentice-Hall of Canada, Ltd., *Toronto*
Prentice-Hall of India Private Limited, *New Delhi*
Prentice-Hall of Japan, Inc., *Tokyo*
Prentice-Hall of Southeast Asia Pte. Ltd., *Singapore*
Whitehall Books Limited, *Wellington, New Zealand*

To my parents

Biography

James Arlin Cooper is a Division Supervisor at Sandia Laboratories, Albuquerque, New Mexico, where he has worked for the past 16 years on electromagnetic theory, radar guidance systems, electronic coded switches, unique signal generators, and unique signal decoders. He is an Adjunct Professor at the University of New Mexico, Albuquerque. Dr. Cooper received the B.S. and M.S. degrees from the University of New Mexico and the Ph.D. degree from Stanford University.

Contents

Preface

The need for a book of this type became apparent to me while working on a microprocessor course for management personnel at Sandia Laboratories.* The participants in the course had a wide variety of backgrounds, but their interest in the exploding technology of microprocessors was uniformly intense. The hunger for information was exemplified by consistent class attendance, searching discussions during class, and eager participation in homework and laboratory exercises. This reaction to the course was gratifying; but more importantly, it was indicative of a need and desire for management personnel to be more informed on this important topic.

Although there are now many books on microprocessors, there seems to be a need for a treatment that is oriented toward a management point of view. This book is written for those persons who need to understand microprocessor basics without becoming expert users; who need to know about the history of the field and its prognosis so that they can put rapidly occurring changes into perspective; who need to understand and make decisions relating to peripheral and laboratory equipment and software aids; who must grasp manpower, equipment, and software costs; and who must have a good conception of the decisions involved in microprocessor usage.

Other unusual and useful features of the book include extensive sections of reference value to managers such as a definitive glossary, a

*The course, "Microprocessors for Managers," was taught to management personnel (Vice Presidents, Directors and Department Managers) at Sandia Laboratories, Albuquerque, New Mexico and Livermore, California locations in early 1979.

"numerology" list, a list of abbreviations, a table of microprocessors on the market today, and performance plots of benchmark programs.

Chapters 1–6 cover fundamental microprocessor concepts and are intended to give a basic understanding of device operations. Chapters 7 and 8 are oriented toward applications in order to show typical uses for microprocessors. Chapters 9–12 provide an examination of topics of special interest to managers. These four chapters very nearly provide a standalone survey unit for readers interested only in management considerations.

Considerable help was provided in bringing together the material for this book. Cliff Harris read, edited, and made numerous suggestions throughout the text. Cliff, with help from Ted Myers and Dennis Eilers, created the illustrative routines in Chapter 7. Karen Winkler's production work (editing, design, and liaison) was skillful, expeditious, and an important contribution.

Other participants included Ashley McConnell, who provided editing and suggestions; Bob Gregory, who was a consultant on integrated circuit technology; and Arlene Dyckes and Irene Garcia, who helped with typing and a variety of tedious tasks. The manuscript was typed by Patt Cooper, Mirium Arnold, Arlene, and Irene. John Shane, Rick Turner, and Larry Nelson assisted in preparing material. The contents of the book were improved by the invigorating classroom interaction with my Sandia Laboratories students.

I greatly appreciate all the help I received and hope that this book reflects, at least to some extent, the excellence of those contributions.

James Arlin Cooper

chapter one

Background

1.1. INTRODUCTION

Microprocessors are the key item in *processor-based digital signal processing systems*, which will be examined in this book. This field has already given evidence of becoming one of the richest, most influential, most exciting areas of scientific and engineering endeavor in history. A unique blend of semiconductor technology, computer hardware and software techniques, and logic design has been evolving at a rapid rate over the past few years. The payoffs in extensive computing power, low cost, and small size would have been unbelievable a decade ago.

Our objectives will be to examine microprocessors and related topics from a manager's point of view. Although the scope will necessarily be limited, the understanding obtained should prove valuable as a basis for making decisions or evaluating decisions pertaining to the use of microprocessors in achieving organizational goals.

Of special interest to managers are such topics as consideration of trade-offs involved in selecting microprocessors as basic system components; selection of the preferable technology, manufacturer, and model; determination of personnel requirements and the extent to which they are involved; evaluation of cost effectiveness of hardware and software laboratory support equipment; and examination of special documentation problems.

Near the end of the book we will prognosticate about future trends in microprocessor-based technology and likely impacts on general technology and our society. There is every reason to believe that these impacts will be profound.

1

1.2. HISTORY

A. Computer Technology

At the beginning of the 1970s, semiconductor technology and computer technology were solidifying an important partnership that yielded the component called a *microprocessor* (see Figure 1.1). Briefly, a microprocessor is a small device that is capable of carrying out "programmed" operations (instructions) in the same fashion as a computer. It is not a computer, or even a "microcomputer," but it does have many of the same central logic functions. These tiny devices quickly had a synergistic impact on the technologies that had given them birth. In addition, they began to cause striking changes in logic design; commercial products, such as games, microwave ovens, and "smart" terminals; and instrumentation. Today, microprocessors are tumbling off semiconductor processing lines at a rate in excess of

Figure 1.1 A microprocessor. This photomicrograph of a microprocessor chip illustrates the complexity of a device actually measuring 4.5 by 5.5 mm. The device shown is a Sandia Laboratories version of the RCA 1802. Courtesy of Sandia Laboratories, Albuquerque, NM.

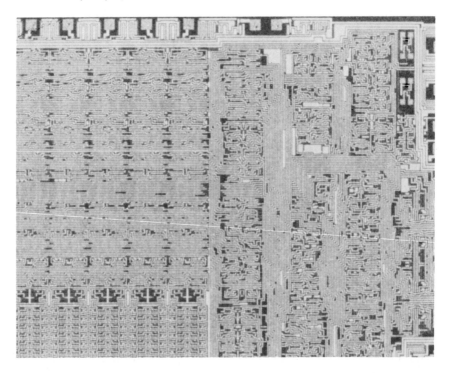

10,000,000 per year. Many microcomputers (computers that use a micro-processor for their central processing unit) are available for less than $1,000, bringing *personal computers* within a reasonable price range. Microprocessors are found in automobiles, service stations, cash registers, children's games, and educational devices. A microprocessor manufacturer (Intel Corporation) claims to have replaced IBM as the world leader in numbers of computer sales.

However, the contrast between microprocessors and large-scale computers is startling. Figure 1.2 shows part of a modern computing facility (at Sandia Laboratories) containing the typical arrays of logic devices, power supplies, consoles, fast access memory, mass storage memory, and operators. A microprocessor is shown in Figure 1.3 situated on a penny. Although a microprocessor also needs peripheral devices and equipment to peform useful tasks, the overall combination of small size, low cost, low power consumption, and high reliability are incredible when the complexity of tasks that can be accomplished with microprocessors is considered.

The sequence of events that led to microprocessors provides an interesting history (see Figure 1.4).

Charles Babbage (1792–1871) proposed a gear-type digital computer in 1833. Babbage was an English mathematician who devoted about 50 years of his life and a considerable amount of his own and others' financial resources to calculating machinery, but his computer was never built. This

Figure 1.2 Portion of the computing facility at Sandia Laboratories. Courtesy of Sandia Laboratories, Albuquerque, NM.

Figure 1.3 Sandia Laboratories version of the RCA 1802 microprocessor (on a penny). Courtesy of Sandia Laboratories, Albuquerque, NM.

is illustrative of the role necessity often plays in technological advances. It was not until World War II that a real need for computers was apparent, although a relay computer was designed at Bell Laboratories in 1937.

The first electronic digital computer was apparently the Colossus, which became operational in 1943 at Bletchley Park, England. It was a 1,500-tube dedicated computer for cryptoanalysis applications. Several computers similar to the first Colossus were built, but a long-lasting cloak of secrecy prevented these devices from contributing significantly to the development of future computers.

In 1943, the ENIAC computer project was begun for the U.S. Army for dedicated ballistic trajectory computations. The project was spear-headed by John Mauchly and J. Presper Eckert of the University of Pennsylvania Moore School of Engineering. The *program* was wired into the machine by plug-in wire interconnections. The ENIAC used about 18,000 vacuum tubes, occupied a 30-ft by 50-ft room, consumed 150 kW of power, and took about 3 years to build—at a cost of $400,000.

Neither the Colossus nor the ENIAC were *stored-program* computers (computers whose program can be "stored" in memory in the same manner

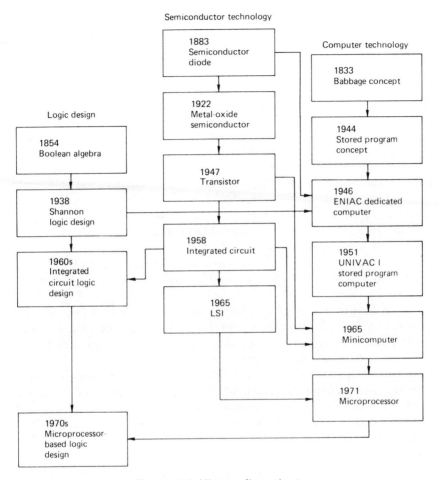

Figure 1.4 History flow chart.

as data). The stored-program (von Neumann[1]) concept was conceived in 1944 and then was built into the UNIVAC I, the first general-purpose commercial computer. The UNIVAC, developed by Remington Rand, used a mercury delay line memory. It gained a special measure of fame by assisting Walter Cronkite in analyzing the 1952 elections.

Transistorized computers, which began to appear in about 1960, had significant improvements in terms of reliability, speed, power consumption,

[1]The common credit to John von Neumann for the stored-program concept is disputed by J. Presper Eckert and John Mauchly.

and size. This soon led to tabletop or rack-mounted computers called *mini-computers* in 1965. The development of microprocessors made *microcomputers* available, these beginning to appear on the market in 1974.

B. Semiconductor Technology

Meanwhile, the semiconductor diode and its capability to perform logic functions had been known since 1883, but systems of the complexity of ENIAC and UNIVAC were not possible until "active" devices were available to provide buffering and drive capabilities as well as logic functions. Vacuum triodes were the active devices used in the first computers.

The invention of the transistor (also an active device) was announced at Bell Laboratories in 1947. This had a major impact on the development of the computer.

By 1958, when transistor usage had begun to generally supplant vacuum-tube usage, the processes that made the integrated circuit possible (including photolithography and solid-state diffusion) became practical. Scientists learned to "batch-process" semiconductor devices on thin *wafers* of germanium or silicon.

An *integrated circuit* consists of an interconnected group of components on a single structure or substrate. The substrate used is almost always silicon because of its nearly ideal electrical properties and because of the relative ease with which it can be processed.

Silicon ingots are grown from a molten vat by inserting a "seed" crystal structure in the vat. As the structure is slowly turned and withdrawn, it develops a relatively large, roughly cylindrical crystalline structure which develops as it is pulled from the vat. This ingot is ground into a cylindrical shape (except for a flat reference edge) and is sawed with a diamond-edged saw into thin slices, or wafers.

The wafers have rectangular integrated circuits processed into their surface with the aid of *photolithography* or a process similar to photolithography. In photolithography, masks are used to selectively introduce processing (deposition of materials and diffusion of controlled impurities) to carefully defined areas of the substrate. This requires a drawing, which can be done by hand for simple integrated circuits but requires computer-aided design for circuits as complex as microprocessors. Figure 1.5 shows the mask detail for a microprocessor. Figure 1.6 shows a wafer containing an array of microprocessors.

Testing is accomplished by *wafer probing* (Figure 1.7) so that bad devices can be marked for deletion from the process. After testing, the wafer is sectioned into individual dice or chips. The chips are assembled into *carriers*, using fine wire bonds to make connections to the chips. The carriers make the contact accessible either directly or by further fan-out into a "dual-in-line package" (DIP) like that shown in Figure 1.8. The device is then sealed by lidding (Figure 1.9) and put through a final test.

Figure 1.5 Photolithography artwork. Courtesy of Sandia Laboratories, Albuquerque, NM.

Figure 1.6 Wafer (approximately 50 mm in diameter and 0.3 mm thick) containing an array of microprocessors. Courtesy of Sandia Laboratories, Albuquerque, NM.

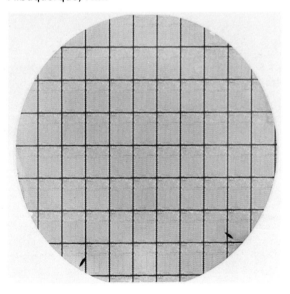

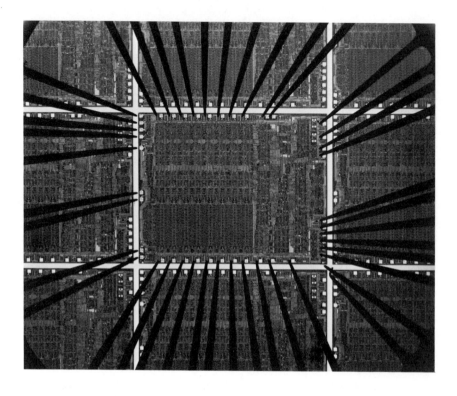

Figure 1.7 Wafer probe testing. Courtesy of Michael E. Justice, Sandia Laboratories, Albuquerque, NM.

Figure 1.8 Chip in dual-in-line package (DIP). Courtesy of Sandia Laboratories, Albuquerque, NM.

Figure 1.9 Chip in lidded dual-in-line package. Courtesy of Sandia Laboratories, Albuquerque, NM.

The first integrated circuits contained single logic devices. Soon a few devices were fabricated on a single substrate structure (*chip*). This became known as *small-scale integration* (SSI). Technological improvements created the capability to make on the order of 100 devices on a chip—*medium-scale integration* (MSI). The trend continued, and by 1969 the capability to make about 1,000 devices per chip existed. *Large-scale integration* (LSI) had arrived. LSI has been the basis of microprocessor development. However, current technology is capable of densities on the order of 100,000 devices on a chip, and the term *very large scale integration* (VLSI) is commonly used to describe this capability.

LSI technology was first applied to memory devices and custom logic chips in the late 1960s. The microprocessor concept was not utilized until 1969.

In 1969, a Japanese calculator manufacturer (Busicom) contacted a U.S. semiconductor manufacturer (Intel Corporation) to work on a design for an unusually flexible (and programmable) calculator chip set. M. E. (Ted) Hoff, who had studied the application of computers to adaptive learning machines at Stanford University a few years previously, was working on the project. Hoff saw a way to simplify Intel's development effort by using computer technology for the application, and got the immediate support of Intel management. Intel proposed using a *central processing unit* (CPU) chip, a *program* (instructions) memory chip, and a *scratch pad* (temporary memory) chip to implement the calculator. The CPU was labeled the 4004 by Intel and it became known as a *microprocessor*. The complexity of the 4004 was roughly equivalent to that of the ENIAC, but it was twenty times as fast, thousands of times more reliable, cost a ten thousandth as much and occupied a thirty thousandth of the volume, as a result of LSI technology (see Table 1.1).

Before the Intel 4004 was announced as a commercial product in 1971, a similar sequence of events took place. A terminal manufacturer, Datapoint, sent a target specification to Intel and Texas Instruments for a

Table 1.1

COMPARISON OF ENIAC AND INTEL 4004

ENIAC Computer	*4004 Microprocessor*
18,000 vacuum tubes	2,250 transistors
30-ft × 50-ft room	3 mm × 4 mm
150 kW power	0.6 W power
Cost $400,000	Cost $5

chip to be used in intelligent terminal applications. This resulted in the development of the successful Intel 8008 microprocessor, announced in 1972. However, the importance of these developments to general logic design was not immediately appreciated.

C. Logic Design

While the development of the microprocessor was taking place, the discipline of logic design was also evolving and interacting with computer and semiconductor technology. In about 1854, a lawyer-mathematician named George Boole had developed *Boolean algebra* as a tool for formalizing thought processes. Boole's work achieved little notice until 1938, when Claude Shannon pointed out its usefulness in designing relay circuits with a capability for performing logic functions. This *switching theory* was soon applied to vacuum-tube circuits and became (and still is) a strong basis for logic design.

As semiconductor technology developed, logic designers progressed from using building blocks ranging from gates and flip flops (see Figure 1.10) to integrated circuits such as counters, read-only memories, coders, decoders, multiplexers, demultiplexers, and programmable logic arrays. The advent of LSI allowed the design of complex chips containing *custom logic*.

However, custom LSI presents economic problems for semiconductor manufacturers. Cost of semiconductors can be minimized by achieving large production runs of standard components. Custom LSI was not attractive for low-volume requirements.

It was about 1973 when the importance of microprocessor-based logic design began to be appreciated. For the logic designer, the microprocessor offered a standard commercial component that could be purchased with confidence that the design had been frozen and well tested. *Second-sourced devices* soon became available. Functions could be rapidly designed by programming. Modification and redesign seldom required changing the basic hardware.

The semiconductor manufacturer was able to dramatically reduce

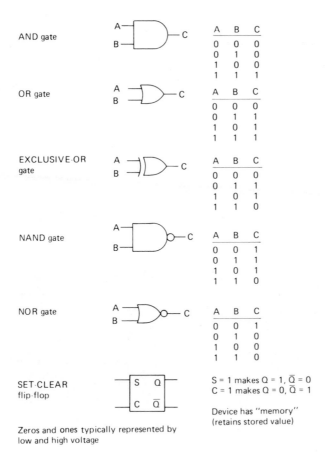

AND gate		A B C
		0 0 0
		0 1 0
		1 0 0
		1 1 1

OR gate		A B C
		0 0 0
		0 1 1
		1 0 1
		1 1 1

EXCLUSIVE-OR gate		A B C
		0 0 0
		0 1 1
		1 0 1
		1 1 0

NAND gate		A B C
		0 0 1
		0 1 1
		1 0 1
		1 1 0

NOR gate		A B C
		0 0 1
		0 1 0
		1 0 0
		1 1 0

SET-CLEAR flip-flop

S = 1 makes Q = 1, $\bar{Q}$ = 0
C = 1 makes Q = 0, $\bar{Q}$ = 1

Device has "memory"
(retains stored value)

Zeros and ones typically represented by low and high voltage

Figure 1.10 Some commonly used logic elements.

chip cost by manufacturing large quantities of standard chips. Since most digital circuit applications were amenable to microprocessor-based design, the potential market was immense. Semiconductor manufacturers rushed to get into the microprocessor business. Today there are hundreds of microprocessor models available. The variety of applications for microprocessors is awesome and is probably only beginning.

BIBLIOGRAPHY

BYLINSKY, GENE, "Here Comes the Second Computer Revolution," *Fortune*, November 1975, p. 134.

ECKERT, J. P., "Thoughts on the History of Computing," *Computer*, December 1976, pp. 58–65.

Microelectronics. San Francisco: W. H. Freeman & Company, 1977.

RANDELL, BRIAN, "Colossus: Godfather of the Computer," *New Scientist*, February 10, 1977.

RANDALL, BRIAN, *The Origins of Digital Computers.* New York: Springer-Verlag, 1973.

chapter two

Basic Principles

2.1. MICROPROCESSOR-BASED SYSTEM ORGANIZATION

A. General System Framework

A fundamental problem facing designers is how to derive desired outputs from available inputs in the most efficient manner possible. Figure 2.1 illustrates this general framework, where the inputs might result from human action, environmental sensors, or direct connection to other systems. Typical outputs would be control connections to other systems, some sort of physical action, or information displays (lights, printing) for human interpretation.

Figure 2.1 General system framework.

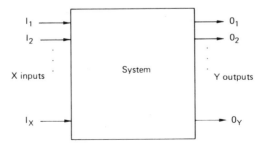

B. Digital Systems

Although the system can usually be realized in a variety of ways (including the use of mechanical devices or analog electronics), digital electronics (electronics for processing digital data) are advantageous where high accuracy, small size, or drift-free operation is required. In order to allow general inputs and outputs, interface circuitry is required (Figure 2.2). Typical interface circuits include keyboards, analog-to-digital (A/D) converters, digital-to-analog (D/A) converters, and level shifters, among others.

Combinational Logic In situations where the m digital outputs in Figure 2.2 are derived exclusively from the n digital inputs, the digital electronics portion is called *combinational logic*. Combinational logic is made up of interconnected *gates*, the output of each depending in some defined fashion on its input. However, in all but the simplest systems, some kind of *memory* is required, so that outputs are based not only on present inputs, but also on a history of past events because of a desire to execute a "sequence" of events.

Sequential Logic Digital electronics systems utilizing memory are called *sequential logic* systems (Figure 2.3). Memory elements are often *flip flops*, which store a *binary digit (bit)*, 0 or 1. The stored value can be changed

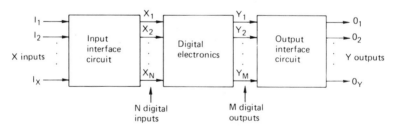

Figure 2.2 Digital system.

Figure 2.3 Sequential logic.

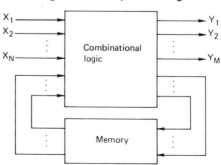

in response to the flip-flop inputs. Techniques for designing sequential logic systems in a fairly straightforward manner have been in use for many years.

Processor-based Systems   Computers can be regarded as a special type of sequential logic system, since they also receive input data and provide output data based on memory. However, they have the additional capabilities of *processor-based logic*, which derives outputs based on inputs, memory, and program control. *Program control* means that a sequence of *instructions* (a program) is executed. Each instruction influences the control of digital data (Figure 2.4). The instructions are commonly stored in a program memory. If the program memory is fixed, the system is commonly called a *controller*. (A *microcontroller* is a microprocessor-based controller.).

The area within the dashed box is the central processing unit (CPU). The CPU might also contain some memory.

The main advantage of program control is that a high degree of flexibility exists within a common system structure or "architecture," since changes can be made by altering program memory, typically a relatively simple task. In many cases, system design by specifying program steps is easier and more natural than ordinary sequential logic design. A disadvantage of processor-based logic is slower speed, because instructions must often be executed sequentially to implement a logic function. Another problem is that the processor circuitry is relatively complex. This degree of complexity might not be justifiable unless it could be used on a large scale.

Figure 2.4 Processor-based logic.

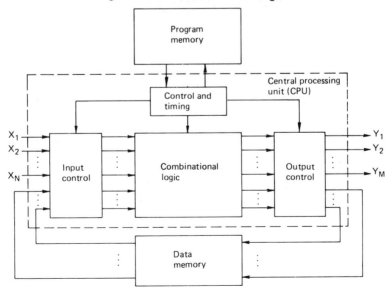

These considerations were important in the development of microprocessors. LSI technology provided the capability to build a complex digital circuit, such as a CPU, on a single chip. These CPU chips (microprocessors) could be mass-produced at a cost of a few dollars a chip, allowing designers of digital logic systems to obtain at a very low cost standard components as the basis for their systems. The desired functions for each application could then be designed largely through *software,*[1] program steps the processor could execute.

A common microprocessor-based architecture (structure arranged from building blocks) is shown in Figure 2.5. The CPU or microprocessor contains circuitry for executing instructions, controlling data flow, making decisions based on tests, temporarily storing data, and performing logic and arithmetic functions. The ROM is a *read-only memory* which is used to store a dedicated program (firmware) and numbers or constants that might be needed during execution. No data can be entered into ROM during program execution. The RAM is a *random-access memory* or *read/write memory* which can store data for use during program execution. In fact, program instructions could be stored in RAM for general purpose or nondedicated applications.

The connection between components in Figure 2.5 is through the use of a *bus,* which is a group of lines on which data and control signals can flow and which are shared by several devices. Access to the bus is most

Figure 2.5 Microprocessor-based system architecture.

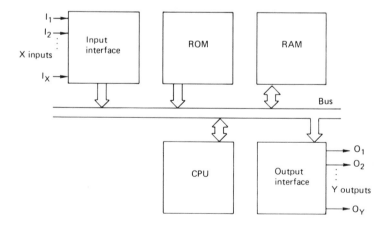

[1]Note the use of "software" to indicate programs as opposed to "hardware," which indicates physical circuits.

often controlled by the CPU so that the intended data source and data destination are connected to the bus at the proper time.[2]

2.2. INTRODUCTION TO PROGRAMMING

Programming is the technique used to convey step-by-step instructions to be executed by a processor in order to perform desired tasks. This requires learning what instructions the processor designers have made available to the user. Wide differences are found among different processors; and, as time passes, differences may even be found for a particular processor. Also, programming languages and levels of languages vary.

The basic programming language that a processor responds to is called *machine language.* Our main interest in this chapter will be in *assembly language,* which is a symbolic form of machine language. Although higher-level languages similar to FORTRAN, ALGOL, or BASIC are sometimes used in microprocessors, detailed understanding of the devices depends on studying machine language or assembly language.[3]

In this section we will discuss a few of the CPU constituents that are crucial to understanding basic program operation. Subsequently, the CPU organization (architecture) will be examined in more detail.

In preparation for studying programming logic, it is appropriate to consider how data in general appear within typical digital system hardware.

A. Digital Data

Digits explicitly appearing in most common digital electronics systems are *binary* (from the base-2 radix number system). This means that only two digits, 0 and 1, are directly represented. The representation can be in terms of two voltage levels (low or high), magnetic flux direction, charge presence, open or closed switches, and so on. The technique most often used in microprocessor-based systems depends on voltage levels.

Binary data are used for simplicity and reliability. It is easier and more reliable to design circuits that produce a voltage above or below a narrow "threshold" region than to struggle with the fine resolutions required for digital systems using a larger radix. Efficiency of representation suffers; it

---

[2]A "microprocessor," as the term is used in this book, can have some amount of ROM or RAM incorporated on the CPU chip. Some authors refer to microprocessor chips that contain ROM and RAM as "microcomputers." We prefer a more rigorous definition of a microcomputer (see Glossary).

[3]Assembly language and higher-level languages require "translators" to convert them to machine language.

takes more binary digits (bits) to represent information; but the current size of digital components makes this consideration relatively unimportant.

Binary representations are used in processor-based systems to represent numbers and instructions. An associated group of bits may represent a *fixed-point* (integer) number, a *floating-point* (scientific notation) number, or a program instruction.

B. Data Organization

For operational efficiency, systems usually process a group of bits of fixed length (a *word*) together. The number of bits processed (called *word length*) generally varies from 4 to 16 in microprocessors, depending on the model, with 8 bits (generally referred to as a *byte*) being the most common at present. If an instruction or piece of data in an 8-bit machine requires more than 8 bits, more than one word (byte) must be processed and combined.

Data appear in memory organized as words with a particular identifier (*location* or *address*) associated with each word. The memory has address inputs and data inputs/outputs. Every operation to insert data into memory (*write*) or to derive data from memory[4] (*read*) is controlled by an address input to identify the location at which the word of data is stored. Figure 2.6 shows examples of a 4-bit organization and an 8-bit organization. The addresses are indicated to the left of each group of digits, and the contents at each address are shown within the boxes.

C. Instructions

The execution of programmed instructions by a processor begins by processor examination (*reading*) of a word or group of words from a particular location or locations in memory, and *decoding* the bit pattern to set up control signals for the task to be done.

Note that until the word is read, instructions and data are indistinguishable (von Neumann concept). Both appear as bit patterns in memory. Usually, a word of the fixed length the processor is designed for is associated with each location. The instruction locations are crucial. The processor is designed to expect its first instruction after turn-on or reset at a particular memory location. This location (usually 0) is "pointed to" by (or stored in) a *program counter* (PC), which furnishes the address input to memory. The PC is incremented to the next instruction address after each instruction is read, unless commanded by program control to point elsewhere.

[4]Read is usually a nondestructive process. That is, reading data from memory leaves memory unaltered.

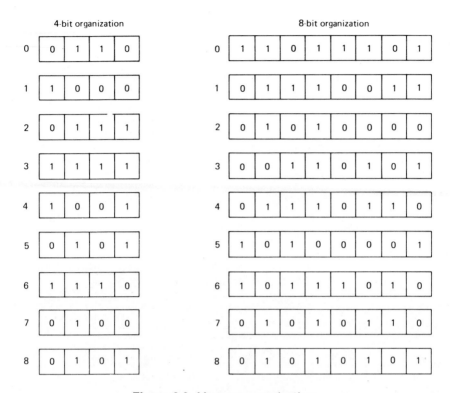

Figure 2.6 Memory organization.

The examination of an instruction word (or words) is achieved through a read process during a processor operation called a *fetch cycle* (see Figure 2.7). A fetch cycle reads a word from memory into a temporary-storage processor register called an *instruction register* (IR). The read takes place from the memory location whose address is contained in (pointed at) by the PC. Decode circuitry is connected to the IR during the processor operation called an *execute cycle,* during which control signals are generated by the decode circuitry. The types of information that might be contained in an instruction code are: (1) operation code (Op-code) for the operation to be performed, (2) address (or addresses) at which an operand (or operands) will be found, (3) address at which resultant data are to be written, and (4) address at which the next instruction can be found (or number from which it can be calculated).

Program execution and programming philosophy can best be understood in four steps: (1) we will give an example of the execution of an individual instruction; (2) we will consider an example of a small segment of a program (a subprogram); (3) we will consider the generation of an entire program; and (4) we will consider the peripheral and housekeeping steps

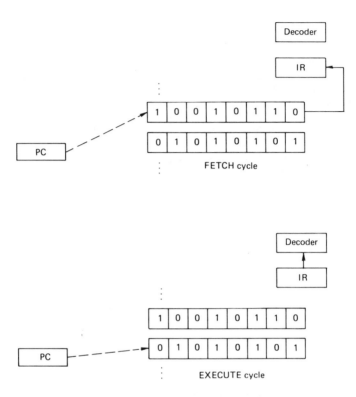

Figure 2.7 Illustration of the fetch and execute cycles.

associated with a program. All of these steps will be presented in a general way at first. Eventually, the user of a microprocessor has to come to grips with the rules for the particular machine.

In preparation for understanding instruction execution, we need to consider the address information mentioned previously that might be contained as part of an instruction. Most microprocessors work with 16-bit addresses. This allows 65,536 addresses (2^{16}), which is usually a sufficient number for program and data storage (see Figure 2.8). An instruction containing 16 bits for address information is usually considered to be a long instruction, so that abbreviated forms are often used. In these cases fewer than 16 bits can be used to represent 16-bit addresses. This will be elaborated on subsequently.

D. Hexadecimal Coding

It is convenient to consider a shorthand representation often used to represent bit patterns, called *hexadecimal coding*. This is simply a conversion of each group of 4 bits into the hexadecimal (base 16) number system. The

Bit representation of address	Decimal equivalent
0 0 0 0 0 0 0 0 0 0 0 0 0 0 0 0	0
0 0 0 0 0 0 0 0 0 0 0 0 0 0 0 1	1
0 0 0 0 0 0 0 0 0 0 0 0 0 0 1 0	2
0 0 0 0 0 0 0 0 0 0 0 0 0 0 1 1	3
0 0 0 0 0 0 0 0 0 0 0 0 0 1 0 0	4
0 0 0 0 0 0 0 0 0 0 0 0 0 1 0 1	5
0 0 0 0 0 0 0 0 0 0 0 0 0 1 1 0	6
0 0 0 0 0 0 0 0 0 0 0 0 0 1 1 1	7
0 0 0 0 0 0 0 0 0 0 0 0 1 0 0 0	8
0 0 0 0 0 0 0 0 0 0 0 0 1 0 0 1	9
0 0 0 0 0 0 0 0 0 0 0 0 1 0 1 0	10
.	.
.	.
.	.
1 1 1 1 1 1 1 1 1 1 1 1 1 1 1 1	65,535

Figure 2.8 Illustration of 16-bit addressing.

conversion can be made directly from 4 bits to one hexadecimal digit since $2^4 = 16$. The 16 hexadecimal symbols conventionally used are 0 through 9 followed by A through F. The code is tabulated in Table 2.1 and reproduced in Appendix D for convenient reference. Figure 2.9 shows the hexadecimal code applied to 16-bit addressing.

Table 2.1

HEXADECIMAL CODING

Bit pattern	Hexadecimal symbol
0000	0
0001	1
0010	2
0011	3
0100	4
0101	5
0110	6
0111	7
1000	8
1001	9
1010	A
1011	B
1100	C
1101	D
1110	E
1111	F

E. Fetch and Execute Control Signals

A basic understanding of logic gates and hexadecimal coding makes possible a concise description of how voltage levels are actually used to control data flow during the fetch and execute cycles. A simplified explanation is illustrated in Figures 2.10 and 2.11. During the fetch cycle (Figure 2.10), the contents of the PC are gated onto the address bus by control signals. The

Bit representation of address	Hexadecimal code
0 0 0 0 0 0 0 0 0 0 0 0 0 0 0 0	0 0 0 0
0 0 0 0 0 0 0 0 0 0 0 0 0 0 0 1	0 0 0 1
.	.
.	.
0 0 0 0 0 0 0 0 0 0 0 0 1 0 1 0	0 0 0 A
.	.
.	.
1 0 1 1 0 1 1 1 1 1 0 0 0 0 1 1	B 7 C 3
.	.
.	.
1 1 1 1 1 1 1 1 1 1 1 1 1 1 1 1	F F F F

Figure 2.9 Hexadecimal coding of 16-bit addresses.

Figure 2.10 Fetch-cycle control signals.

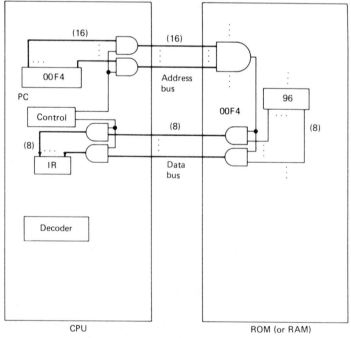

22

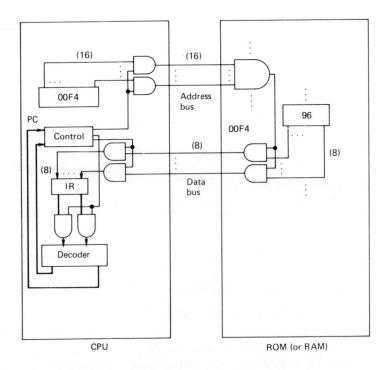

Figure 2.11 Execute-cycle control signals.

16-bit pattern is decoded in the memory to excite a particular location, whose contents are gated onto the data bus and transferred to the IR by control signal gating. The address and data flow are indicated by the heavy lines. During the execute cycle (Figure 2.11), control signals gate the instruction code from the IR to the decoder, which in turn generates control intelligence corresponding to the instruction fetched from memory. The flow of instruction data is indicated by the heavy lines.

F. Fundamental CPU Registers

In carrying out instructions, some common CPU *registers* (temporary storage locations for groups of bits) and circuit components are often utilized. Some of these are shown in Figure 2.12. The role of the PC, IR, decoder, and control circuits has been briefly discussed previously. The *arithmetic logic unit* does fundamental arithmetic and logic operations, such as add, subtract, and shift. Its results are placed in the *accumulator*. The *M register* is a memory pointer or data pointer often used to identify a data location in the same way that the PC identifies an instruction location.

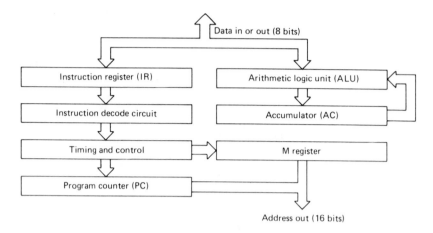

Figure 2.12 CPU constituents involved in instruction example.

G. Example Instruction Execution

As an example of the instruction execution process, assume that a program is being carried out on an 8-bit processor (a processor that processes data in 8-bit words). Assume an 8-bit accumulator (AC) for temporary storage of operands and 16-bit addresses. The processor will be assumed to have a 16-bit M register pointing at memory for operands and a 16-bit PC pointing at an address in program memory for its next instruction. Assume that instructions or data at a particular address consist of 8 bits (a byte). The fetch process reads the data from the memory location pointed at by the PC into the *instruction register* (IR). This information is decoded by the instruction decode circuit and acted on by the timing and control circuit. Assume that the instruction code signifies "add (in binary) the contents of the location specified by the M register to the number stored in the AC and leave the result in the AC." During the execute cycle, an operand will be read from the memory location specified by the M register, the operand (number) will be added to the number in the accumulator, and the result will be left in the AC.

For example, assume that the PC contains 000A[5] prior to the instruc-

[5]For example: 000A is a hexadecimal symbol decoded as follows:

$$
\begin{aligned}
0 \quad &= 0000 \\
0 \quad &= \quad\;\; 0000 \\
0 \quad &= \quad\quad\;\; 0000 \\
A \quad &= \quad\quad\quad\;\; 1010 \\
\hline
000A \quad &= 0000000000001010
\end{aligned}
$$

tion fetch; address 000A in memory contains 86, which is the instruction code for "add (in binary) the contents of the location specified by the M register to the number stored in the AC and leave the result in the AC"; the AC contains 87, M contains 076C, and address 076C in memory contains 1B. After execution the AC will contain A2, a hexadecimal representation of the sum of 87 and 1B, and the PC will have incremented one address. This process is shown in Figures 2.13 through 2.15 and is summarized in Table 2.2. The heavy lines in Figures 2.14 and 2.15 correspond to data flow.

Figure 2.13 Outline of example addition operation.

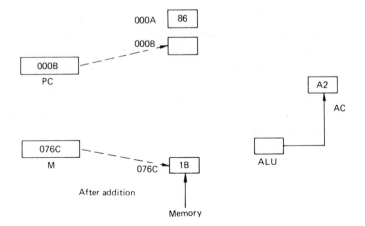

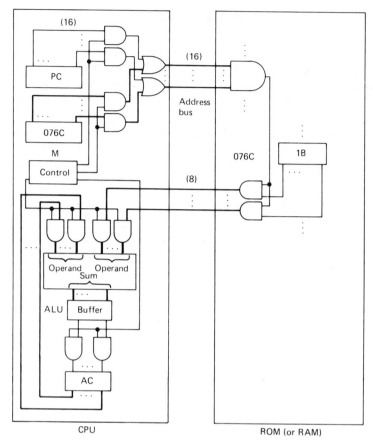

Figure 2.14 Data flow during addition.

H. Flow-Chart Basics

A sequence of program statements can often be planned by means of a *flow chart* or logic diagram showing the processing steps to be taken. Subsequently, the flow chart can be converted to some programming language (e.g., assembly language).

The basic conventions for flow charts are to put programming steps in rectangular boxes, and tests for decision points in diamond-shaped boxes, with arrows indicating the sequence of events (see Figure 2.16). Refinements will be discussed later.

I. Example of a Programmed Operation

As an example problem, assume that two 64-bit numbers to be added (binary addition) are in the memory of an 8-bit processor with 16-bit addresses. The first number begins (least significant portion) with 8 bits at address

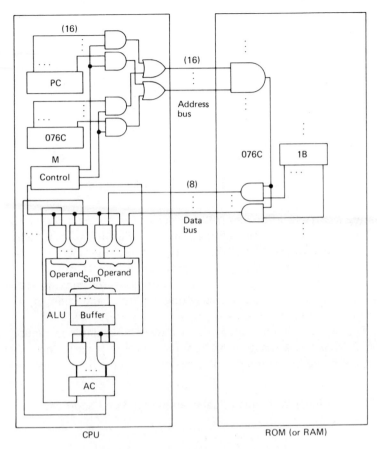

Figure 2.15 Data flow after addition.

Table 2.2

REGISTER AND MEMORY CONTENTS FOR ADDITION EXAMPLE
(NUMBERS IN PARENTHESES ARE HEXADECIMAL)

Location	Contents before fetch		Contents after execution	
AC	10000111	(87)	10100010	(A2)
M	0000011101101100	(076C)	0000011101101100	(076C)
000A	10000110	(86)	10000110	(86)
076C	00011011	(1B)	00011011	(1B)
PC	0000000000001010	(000A)	0000000000001011	(000B)

(hexadecimal) 0100 and is stored in eight locations running through address 0107. The second number (64 bits) is stored in locations 0108 through 010F. The sum is to replace the first number at locations 0100 through 0107. The processor has an "add to accumulator" instruction similar to the one in the previous example with the exception that an addition carry is also provided,

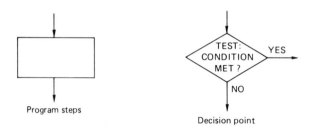

Program steps

Decision point

Figure 2.16 Basic flow-chart symbols.

by setting a carry flip flop (controllable device for storing a binary digit) to "1" if a carry results during addition. The carry-flip-flop value is then added to the least significant digit in the subsequent addition operation. Assume that the processor also has an 8-bit scratch pad register called register C. Assume that the processor also has instructions for moving data into registers, incrementing and decrementing registers, and changing the PC depending on tests of registers.

The problem is illustrated with a numerical example in Figure 2.17. Figure 2.18 shows a diagram of how the addition is performed. The sequences of bit additions indicated by heavy lines in the figure illustrates how

Figure 2.17 Numerical example for 64-bit addition.

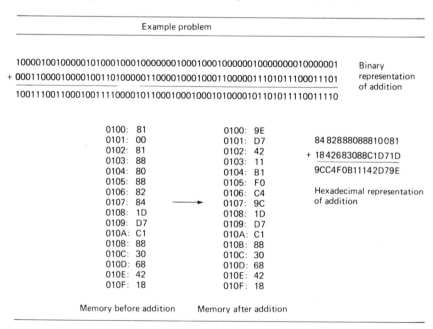

Example problem

1000010010000010100010001000000010001000100000010000000010000001 Binary
+ 0001100001000010011010000011000010001000110000011101011100011101 representation
of addition
1001110011000100111100001011000100010001010000101101011110011110

0100: 81	0100: 9E	84 82888088810081
0101: 00	0101: D7	+ 1842683088C1D71D
0102: 81	0102: 42	9CC4F0B11142D79E
0103: 88	0103: 11	
0104: 80	0104: B1	
0105: 88	0105: F0	
0106: 82	0106: C4	Hexadecimal representation
0107: 84 →	0107: 9C	of addition
0108: 1D	0108: 1D	
0109: D7	0109: D7	
010A: C1	010A: C1	
010B: 88	010B: 88	
010C: 30	010C: 30	
010D: 68	010D: 68	
010E: 42	010E: 42	
010F: 18	010F: 18	

Memory before addition   Memory after addition

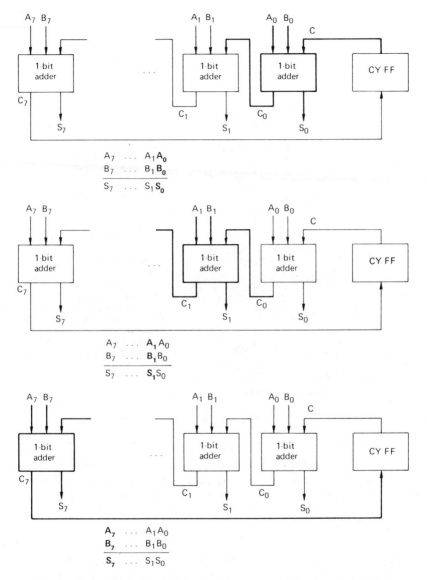

Figure 2.18 Illustration of 8-bit addition utilizing carry flip flop.

the carry flip flop is used as an input in the least significant bit of the addition and as output storage for any carry generated.

The sequence of events necessary to solve the problem is outlined by a flow chart in Figure 2.19. First, registers that serve as pointers to memory for operands and a counter to keep track of the number of additions necessary are set. Also, the carry flip flop is cleared.

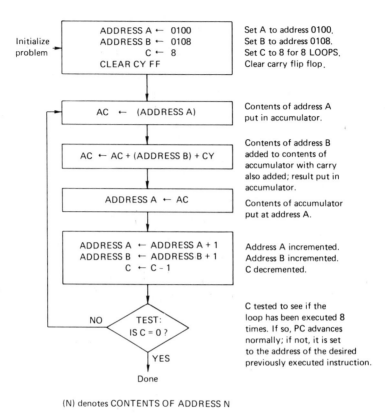

Figure 2.19 Flow chart for adding two 64-bit numbers.

Next, a *loop* is entered. Loops will be given more definitive consideration later; however, the basic intent of a loop is to repetitively use the same instructions a number of times to avoid the large amount of program memory (and programming effort) that would be required if the instructions were repeated in memory. This requires a test (e.g., of a counter) to determine when the loop should be terminated.

Within the loop shown, the AC is loaded with one operand. (The brackets indicate that the *contents* of address A are to be used rather than the address itself.) Next, the contents of address B are added (with carry condition accounted for), and the result is returned to address A. Addresses A and B are incremented to point at the next 8 bits of the operands, and register C is decremented to account for a *pass* through the loop. The ensuing test will give the answer "yes" if we have completed eight passes; if not, control is returned to the beginning of the loop.

This program ignores the final carry that might be generated upon adding the most significant digits. In practice, this carry would probably be stored for future reference or use in the same way the sum was stored. However, since the intent of the example problem was only to illustrate a sequence of instructions to accomplish a task, this routine, but important detail was omitted from the example. This example is programmed at the end of Chapter 4, with the carry stored.

2.3. GENERAL CENTRAL PROCESSING UNIT ARCHITECTURE

Before further consideration of programming, it is useful to probe more deeply into the architecture or structure of the CPU and associated components.

CPU architecture varies widely, but some features are commonly used. Our initial approach will be to establish a general structure without being definitive about particular microprocessors. The variety of features one finds in practice should be kept in mind and will be discussed when appropriate. Some common registers and a common architecture are shown in Figure 2.20.

Some comments are appropriate:

1. Although the architecture shown is for an 8-bit microprocessor (the most common word length used), basic microprocessors exist that use 4, 8, 12, and 16 bits. Another type of microprocessor is called a *bit-slice* microprocessor. These are intended to be concatenated or strung together to give almost arbitrary word-size capability. Bit-slice microprocessors most commonly exist with 2 or 4 bits, allowing processors with word lengths that are multiples of 2 or 4 bits.

2. A 16-bit address bus (the most commonly used size) is shown; other address sizes are in use. The small size of microprocessor chips is a mixed benefit because microprocessors are "pin-limited." In other words, the number of connections that can be made to the chip is limited. This influences the size of buses. Some microprocessors *multiplex* data (switch groups of data in succession) onto buses in order to minimize the number of pin connections on the CPU that must be dedicated to buses. In the architecture shown, 16 pins must be used for the address bus and 8 for the data bus. Power supply connections, control connections, and input/output connections generally use the remaining pins.

3. The *status register* contains bits reflecting the result of the last operation involving the accumulator,[6] allowing tests to be executed. Example conditions represented in the status register are positive or negative,

---

[6]Typical accumulator operations are binary addition, BCD (binary-coded decimal) addition, subtraction, exclusive-OR, inclusive-OR, logical AND, shift (right or left), and complement. Some microprocessors have more operations than these, some fewer.

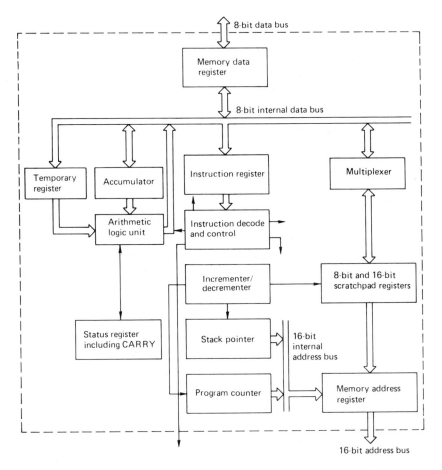

Figure 2.20 Example of CPU architecture.

zero, odd or even "parity" (number of 1's), and "carry" (extra bit generated by addition, subtraction, or shifting).

4. The *stack pointer* designates a position in memory where a series of locations can be used to store data for later retrieval. The usefulness of this concept will be explored further when we consider subroutines.

5. The control portion of a CPU either contains a *clock circuit* or has provisions for an external clock input. A clock is a circuit for delivering regular timed signals that serve as the timekeeping mechanism for the processor. Each event in a sequence occurs in synchronization with the next "clock time" or in response to a signal controlled by the clock and various forms of logic. Microprocessors typically take several clock periods to accomplish a fetch and several more for execution, so that an instruction cycle may contain on the order of 10 to 20 clock cycles.

6. The *memory address register* (MAR) is a buffer register for temporarily storing addresses prior to putting them on the address bus.

7. The *memory data register* (MDR) is a buffer register for temporarily storing data received from memory or about to be sent to memory.

8. Internal buses are generally used within the CPU for transferring instructions, data, and control signals in a manner analogous to external bus connections.

9. *Scratch pad registers* on the CPU chip are generally more readily available in terms of execution time and accessing efficiency than general memory. They play an important role in instruction execution.

A general instruction list is given in Table 2.3. The instructions are not for any particular microprocessor, nor do they necessarily form a comprehensive set, but are merely indicative of the types of operations that can be programmed. Eight-bit words and 16-bit addresses are assumed. Each instruction would have a unique bit pattern for its representation. Mnemonic (alphabetic) coding would also be associated with each instruction for user convenience, similar to the abbreviations given.

Table 2.3
EXAMPLE INSTRUCTION LIST

1. *Move contents of register R to register S (mnemonic abbreviation M R S).*

   This transfers data from one register to another. R and S are symbolic indications that would be replaced by specific bit patterns representing particular registers in an actual instruction. Each register is assumed to contain 1 byte (8 bits).

   This instruction can be applied to scratch pad registers, to the accumulator, to the memory pointer register (M register), and to the stack pointer. However, movement involving 16-bit registers such as the M register and the stack pointer (and sometimes scratch pad registers) must be accomplished 1 byte at a time. Movement involving the least significant byte of these registers must be accomplished in a separate instruction from movement involving the most significant byte. The two portions of these registers must also be named uniquely, such as M0 for the least significant byte of the M register and M1 for the most significant byte.

2. *Load register R with the subsequent byte of data (LD R XX).*

   This causes specified data to be inserted into a designated register or into the accumulator. Generally, a 2-byte instruction is necessary where decoding the first (Op-code) byte from memory conveys to the processor the information that a second (data) byte must be read to complete the instruction. The XX symbol stands for two arbitrary hexadecimal digits that can be chosen for data.

3. *Load accumulator from memory (LAM).*

   This transfers data from the memory location being pointed at by the M register (memory register or data pointer) to the accumulator.

Table 2.3 (continued).

4 . *Store accumulator in memory (SAM).*

This transfers data from the accumulator to the memory location being pointed at by the M register.

5. *Increment register R (IN R).*

This causes the contents of the specified register to be incremented (count increased by 1). An increment from all ones (FF) changes the count to all zeros (00).

6. *Decrement register R (DC R).*

This causes the contents of the specified register to be decremented (count decreased by 1). A decrement from all zeros (00) changes the count to all ones (FF).

7. *Add (ADD).*

This causes a binary addition of two operands, where one operand is in the accumulator and the other is in memory at a location being pointed at by the M register. The result is placed in the accumulator; the carry flip flop is set to 1 if a carry is generated from the most significant digit, and to 0 if not.

8. *Add with carry (ADC).*

This causes a binary addition involving three operands. One operand is in the accumulator; one is in memory at a location being pointed at by the M register; and the third is the bit contained in the carry flip flop, which is added to the least significant position. The carry flip flop is commonly used to facilitate multiple-word (concatenated) additions.

9. *Subtract (SUB).*

This causes a binary subtraction of an operand in memory at a location pointed at by the M register from the contents of the accumulator. The carry flip flop is set to 0 if there is a borrow propagated from the most significant digit and to 1 if not.

10. *Subtract with borrow (SBB).*

This causes a binary subtraction of an operand in memory from the accumulator and also incorporates the carry flip flop into the subtraction in the least-significant-bit position. The carry flip flop is commonly used as a "borrow" indicator to facilitate multiple word (concatenated) subtractions.

11. *Shift left (SHL).*

The contents of the accumulator are shifted left one position, with the most significant digit of the accumulator going to the carry flip flop.

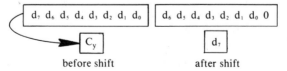

before shift	after shift

Table 2.3 (continued).

12. *Ring shift left (RSL)*

The contents of the accumulator are shifted left one position, with the most significant digit of the accumulator going to the carry flip flop and the contents of the carry flip flop going to the least significant position of the accumulator.

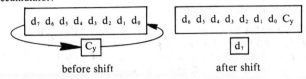

before shift   after shift

13. *Shift right (SHR)*.

The contents of the accumulator are shifted right one position, with the least significant digit of the accumulator going to the carry flip flop.

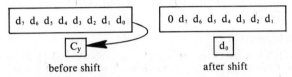

before shift   after shift

14. *Ring shift right (RSR)*.

The contents of the accumulator are shifted right one position, with the least significant digit of the accumulator going to the carry flip flop and the contents of the carry flip flop going to the most significant position of the accumulator.

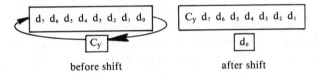

before shift   after shift

15. *Jump (JMP XXXX)*.

This resets the PC to the address specified in the succeeding 2 bytes. The 3-byte instruction can cause a transfer to any address in memory (any program step). The 2 bytes are signified by the XXXX hexadecimal digits.

16. *Jump on zero (JPZ XXXX)*.

This 3-byte instruction resets the PC to the address specified in the succeeding 2 bytes if the accumulator contains zero. If not, the PC increments over these bytes to the next instruction in sequence. The 2 bytes are signified by the XXXX hexadecimal digits.

17. *Jump on no zero (JNZ XXXX)*.

This 3-byte instruction resets the PC to the address specified in the succeeding 2 bytes if the accumulator does not contain zero. If it does, the PC increments over these bytes to the next instruction in sequence. The 2 bytes are signified by the XXXX hexadecimal digits.

Table 2.3 (continued).

18. *Jump on carry (JPC XXXX).*

    This 3-byte instruction resets the PC to the address specified in the succeeding 2 bytes if the carry flip flop contains 1. If not, the PC increments over these bytes to the next instruction in sequence. The 2 bytes are signified by the XXXX hexadecimal digits.

19. *Jump on no carry (JNC XXXX).*

    This 3-byte instruction resets the PC to the address specified in the succeeding 2 bytes if the carry flip flop contains zero. If not, the PC increments over these bytes to the next instruction in sequence. The 2 bytes are signified by the XXXX hexadecimal digits.

20. *Short Jump (SJP XX).*

    This resets the low-order (least significant) byte of the PC to the value specified by the succeeding byte. This 2-byte instruction can cause a transfer of the PC to one of 256 addresses, specified by the XX representation.

21. *Skip Jump (SKX).*

    This causes the PC to add X counts to its normal incremented value, thereby skipping X memory locations. X is symbolic of a hexadecimal digit that may be chosen.

22. *Halt (HLT).*

    This stops processing, for example at the end of a program.

BIBLIOGRAPHY

BARNA, ARPAD, AND DAN PORAT, *Introduction to Microcomputers and Microprocessors.* New York: John Wiley & Sons, Inc., 1976.

HILBURN, JOHN, AND PAUL JULICH, *Microcomputers/Microprocessors.* Englewood Cliffs, N.J.: Prentice-Hall, Inc., 1976.

LEVENTHAL, L. A., *Introduction to Microprocessors.* Englewood Cliffs, N.J.: Prentice-Hall, Inc., 1978.

McGLYNN, DANIEL, *Microprocessors.* New York: John Wiley, & Sons, Inc., 1976.

PEATMAN, J. B. *Microcomputer-based Design.* New York: McGraw-Hill Book Company, 1977.

RAO, G. V., *Microprocessors and Microcomputer Systems.* New York: Van Nostrand Reinhold Company, 1978.

VERONIS, A., *Microprocessors: Design and Applications.* Reston, Va.: Reston, Publishing Co., Inc., 1978.

chapter three

Data and Instruction Processing

3.1. ADDRESSING MODES

A. Discussion

Before we pursue a more complete and detailed understanding of micro-processor programming, it is important to consider addressing modes and memory structure. *Addressing* is the processor action of determining the location where data are to be written or from which data are to be read.

Various addressing schemes are used to improve addressing efficiency. For example, adding two numbers stored in memory might require that we specify the addresses for each number, specify the address where the result should be placed, and specify the address from which the next instruction is to be obtained. If 16 bits are required for each of these pieces of information, a large amount (64 bits) of program memory would be associated with addressing. For this reason, addressing shortcuts are used, such as the use of "pointer" registers in the CPU that can be readily modified. The PC (program counter) register is an example of this type of pointer. The PC is routinely incremented by the CPU for pointing to (specifying the location of) the next instruction, since we expect by convention to find the next instruction at the subsequent address.

Other shortcuts involve arranging data that are to be operated on sequentially in sequential memory locations, "sharing" locations so that the source of one operand is the same as the destination of the result, and using "offsets" from a known address to save bits.

The addressing modes described in this section are various methods used in microprocessors to improve overall program efficiency. Typically many, but not all, of the modes are available for a particular microprocessor. The mode for a particular instruction is explicitly specified by the Op-code translation.

B. Types of Addressing

Accumulator Addressing   This addressing mode is almost universally used in processors. The mode requires that one operand already be in the accumulator. A few microprocessors (e.g., Motorola 6800, National PACE, Signetics 2650) have the added complication of using more than one accumulator. An example chosen from Table 2.3 is ADD, where one of the addition operands is to be found in the accumulator. Note that multiple addressing modes may be found in the same instruction, as is the case for ADD.

Direct Addressing   In the direct addressing mode, the required address is part of the instruction. For an 8-bit processor this mode requires a three-word instruction, since the address requires two words. This mode can be used in almost all microprocessors. An example chosen from Table 2.3 is JMP, illustrated in Figure 3.1. Here a "jump" is executed to the address specified by the two bytes following the instruction.

Figure 3.1 Direct addressing example.

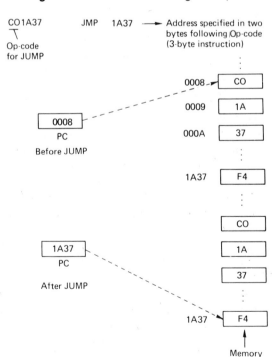

Register Direct Addressing In this mode of addressing, operand data are found in a processor register (or data destination is a register) rather than in ROM or RAM memory. The Op-code determines which register is used. An example chosen from Table 2.3 is INR, where the specified register is to be incremented. This is illustrated in Figure 3.2, with register 4 chosen for incrementing.

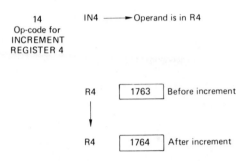

Figure 3.2 Register direct addressing example.

"Paged" Direct Addressing Page addressing is a technique for dividing the entire memory into sections (pages) so that a full address is unnecessary as long as the page does not change. Typically, a page has 256 (2^8) addresses. For a total address space of 2^{16} addresses, this results in 256 pages. The bits required to locate an address on a page are the least significant bits of the address. If page addressing is used for an operand, a *page register* is necessary to store the most significant 8 bits of the address. If page addressing is used in a *jump* instruction (changing the normal PC sequence), the least significant 8 bits of the address are given in the instruction to indicate the location on the page stored in the page register. If *page-zero* addressing is used, the most significant 8 bits are understood to be zero. Generalizing, the total number of bits is not limited to 16 and the number of bits used for the address within a page is not limited to 8.

A typical page structure is outlined in Figure 3.3. An example chosen from Table 2.3 is SJP (short jump), which is illustrated in Figure 3.4.

Relative Addressing In the relative addressing mode, an *offset* address is specified for addition to or subtraction from the PC. An example from Table 2.3 is SKX (skip jump), which is illustrated in Figure 3.5. Although relative addressing is slightly more difficult to implement in CPU circuitry than is paged direct addressing, it gives the user the advantage of not having to worry about page boundaries. If in the example above the PC had been at 17FF, for example, paged direct addressing could not have been used to jump the next two locations, but relative addressing could have been.

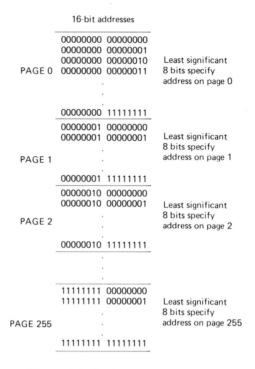

16-bit addresses

	00000000 00000000	
	00000000 00000001	
	00000000 00000010	Least significant
PAGE 0	00000000 00000011	8 bits specify
	.	address on page 0
	.	
	.	
	00000000 11111111	
	00000001 00000000	
	00000001 00000001	Least significant
		8 bits specify
PAGE 1	.	address on page 1
	.	
	00000001 11111111	
	00000010 00000000	
	00000010 00000001	Least significant
	.	8 bits specify
PAGE 2	.	address on page 2
	.	
	00000010 11111111	
	.	
	.	
	.	
	11111111 00000000	
	11111111 00000001	Least significant
	.	8 bits specify
PAGE 255	.	address on page 255
	11111111 11111111	

Figure 3.3 Typical page structure.

Indirect Addressing Indirect addressing specifies the location where the address can be found. The operation is complex and requires a preliminary operation to fetch the address of the data before fetching the data. However, it is useful in applications in which the user wants to change effective addresses without changing instructions. For example, consider the problem outlined in Figure 3.6.

In this example, program memory contains a sequence of instructions for processing an array of data. If the operator wants to use the same set of instructions to process more than one array of data, program memory can use an indirect address to specify the array starting points. Location 1000 should be loaded with the starting address of the array to be processed. In the example, the address of the first array (2000) would be written into location 1000 before the first array was processed; then the address of the second array (3000) would be written into location 1000 before the second array was processed. This process avoids moving an entire array of data by simply moving its address.

Indirect addressing has additional flexibility by virtue of the common use of ROM, thereby making instructions and any specified addresses permanent. The use of indirect addressing allows changing these addresses in RAM. Table 2.3 has no instructions that use indirect addressing.

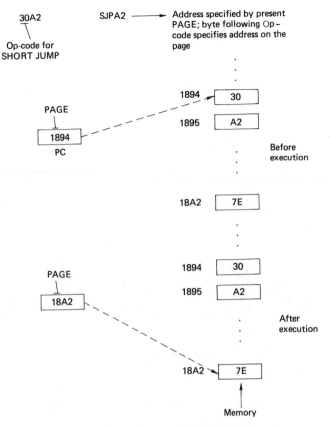

Figure 3.4 Paged direct addressing example.

Register Indirect Addressing Register indirect addressing is similar to indirect addressing. However, the instruction specifies a register in the CPU where the address is stored. This is a popular type of addressing in microprocessors. It is faster than ordinary indirect addressing because one fetch of data from memory is saved.

Prior to using this type of instruction, the CPU register used must be loaded with the required address. An example from Table 2.3 is SUB (subtract), as shown in Figure 3.7.

Indexed Addressing Microprocessors that use indexed addressing (the Motorola 6800 is an example) have *index registers*. Specifying an indexed address by an instruction Op-code results in the contents of the index register being added to the address specified in the instruction to obtain an effective address. Since the index register is easily loaded or modified by the CPU, this allows flexibility for fixed-address instructions stored in ROM. This is especially useful when an array of data must be handled. For example, if the arrays of data shown in Figure 3.6 are to be averaged, each piece

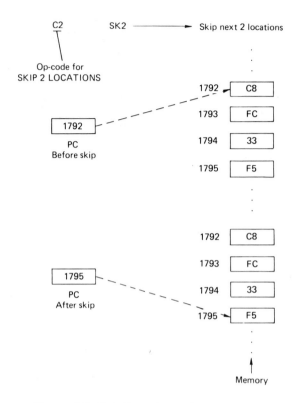

Figure 3.5 Relative addressing example.

Program memory (ROM)	Date memory (RAM)	
Indirect address 1000 is specified as starting point for an array of data	Array of data starting at address 2000	Array of data starting at address 3000
	Location 1000 _____	

Figure 3.6 Illustration of indirect addressing.

of data must be added to accumulate an overall sum. A single indexed add instruction allows this sequence to be accomplished by starting with an addition from the first address and incrementing the index register after each add operation. Table 2.3 has no instructions that use indexed addressing.

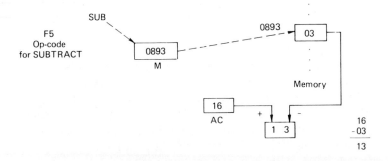

Figure 3.7 Register indirect addressing example.

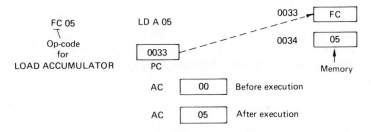

Figure 3.8 Immediate addressing example.

Immediate Addressing   In this mode, the data to be used by an instruction are part of the instruction. In 8-bit microprocessors, this means that the second byte of the instruction (if an 8-bit number is to be acted upon) or the second and third bytes (for a 16-bit number) are programmed data. This is useful for loading data registers or address registers. An example from Table 2.3 is LD A XX (load accumulator). This is illustrated in Figure 3.8.

Stack Addressing   In stack addressing, the address to be used in the instruction is contained in a register called the *stack pointer*. This type of addressing is useful in subroutines, to be discussed later.

3.2. SEMICONDUCTOR MEMORIES

Memories for processor-based systems fall into three general categories: (1) fast-access-speed memories used for immediate interaction with the processor during instruction execution; (2) medium-access-speed memories.

where fast interaction is less imperative; and (3) slow-access-speed memories, where large amounts of data are involved and time is relatively unimportant.

The ROM and RAM applications discussed in Chapters 1 and 2 are examples requiring fast-access-speed memories. Semiconductor memories and core memories fall into this class. Program libraries and data files are often stored in slow-access-speed memories, such as magnetic tape, cassette tape, disk, floppy disk, or drums. Medium-access-speed memories are magnetic bubble devices and charge-coupled devices (CCDs).

Before about 1970, most computer fast-access memories were based on magnetic cores. Although semiconductor memories were available in the late 1960s, they were too expensive for mass-memory applications. Now the cost picture has changed drastically, and semiconductor memories are the mainstay of microprocessor-based systems. They typically give faster read/write access than do magnetic cores, are smaller, cheaper, and use less power. Our emphasis will be almost exclusively on semiconductor memories. Various types of semiconductor memories will be discussed in this section, including ROMs, RAMs, PROMs, EPROMs, and EAROMs.

A. Read-Only Memories

Read-only memories (ROMs) are used to store fixed data and dedicated programs. They are organized into groups of bits (words) stored at each memory location. For example, a 1,024 × 8 ROM has 1,024 addresses, each containing 8 bits.[1] These memories have random access, where any address specification gives access to the eight bit-storage positions at that location. A ROM has address lines for specifying a memory location, an internal decoder, a memory array, data lines for data to be read out, and power and control lines. This is shown as a general concept in Figure 3.9, and with a specific configuration in Figure 3.10.

In Figure 3.9, p input bits are shown, which allows definition of 2^p distinct addresses. If each address contains m bits of information, the memory is said to be an $n \times m$ ROM, where $n = 2^p$. In the example shown, $p = 10$ and $m = 8$, giving a 1,024 × 8 (1K × 8) ROM.

However, a microprocessor with 16 address bits is not directly compatible with a 1K × 8 ROM. An actual device allows for this discrepancy with a *chip enable* input, as shown in Figure 3.10. Additional logic is required to decode the other 6 address bits and to deliver the chip enable signal. This chip enable selects the portion of memory contained in the illustrated chip. The decoder to accomplish this task is a combinational logic

[1]Multiples of 1,024 are often abbreviated K. For example, a 1,024 × 8 ROM can be called a 1K × 8 ROM; 64K addresses represents 65,536 addresses (64 times 1,024); and so on.

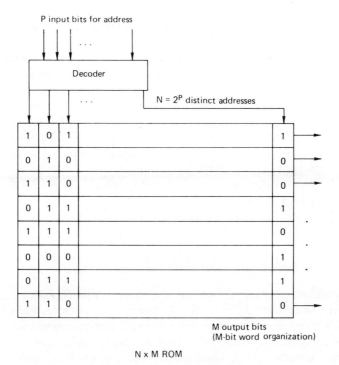

Figure 3.9 Basic ROM structure.

Figure 3.10 Typical ROM.

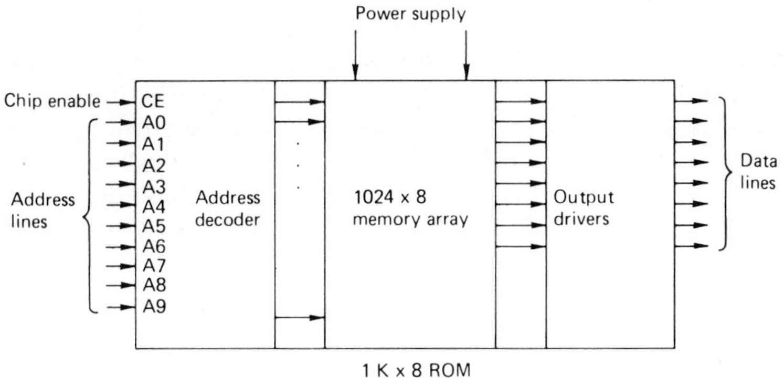

device that either can be added to the collection of devices making up the microprocessor-based system or can be part of a general-purpose *interface* chip. In addition, a decoder is incorporated as part of the ROM circuitry in order to convert the address input to a gating signal to put data from the selected address on the data lines.

ROMs are programmed (data inserted) by the manufacturer, using the customer's specification for bits (usually delivered in a hexadecimal code). Since data insertion is one of the last manufacturing steps, the time for a program to be implemented in ROM is relatively short (approximately 15 weeks). However, the charge for programming ROMs may be in the $1,000 range. ROMs are called *nonvolatile* memory elements since they do not lose data when power is cut off.

ROMs generally have more bits per chip than other semiconductor memories, have low power consumption, and fast (≈ 1 μs) access.

B. Random-Access Memories

Random-access memories (RAMs) are more properly called read/write memories, since data can be written into or read from them. Their random-access characteristic is not unique; most semiconductor memories can have any memory location accessed during a read or write operation.[2] RAM memory is usually *volatile* (data are lost when power is cut off). RAM access times are generally in the vicinity of 100 ns.

RAM circuitry is more complex than ROM circuitry largely because of the added capability required to read or write data. RAM memory is often implemented on multiple chips; sometimes eight RAM chips may be used to implement a memory of 8-bit words, each chip furnishing 1 bit of the word. This type of structure is shown in Figure 3.11.

Figure 3.12 shows a possible 256 × 8 RAM organization. Since there are only eight address lines and most microprocessors use 16-bit addresses, additional logic is necessary to deliver the chip enable signal if this portion of memory is to be addressed.

The enable output and write signals specify whether a read or a write operation is taking place. In the write mode, data are accepted on the data lines and gated into the selected address. In the read mode, the enable output signal is gated to the amplifier control, allowing data from the selected address to be put on the data lines. The amplifiers are called *tristate* bus drivers or *three-state buffers* because they can generate a "high"-voltage output or a "low"-voltage output when turned on by the amplifier control;

---

[2]"Random access" is used as opposed to "sequential access" to distinguish between memories that can have any location accessed during a read or write cycle, and shift registers, (for example, whose memory can only be accessed as bits are shifted out of the end position.

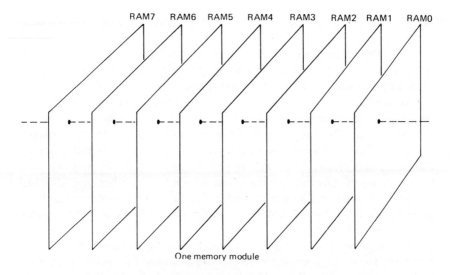

RAM7 RAM6 RAM5 RAM4 RAM3 RAM2 RAM1 RAM0

One memory module

Figure 3.11 Use of eight RAMs to form a module.

Figure 3.12 Typical RAM.

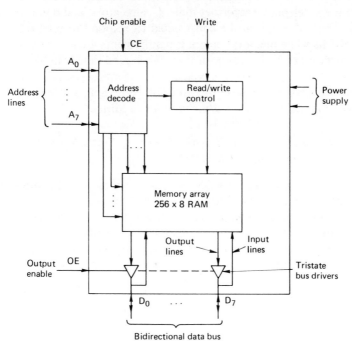

Chip enable   Write

CE

A_0

Address lines

A_7

Address decode

Read/write control

Power supply

Memory array
256 x 8 RAM

Output lines   Input lines

Output enable   OE

Tristate bus drivers

D_0 ... D_7

Bidirectional data bus

and they assume a high-impedance or "open" state when data are not being read out.

RAMs fall into two general classes: static RAMs and dynamic RAMs. *Static* RAMs retain memory as long as power is applied; *dynamic* RAMs must be periodically (every few milliseconds) "refreshed." The *refresh* process is necessary in dynamic RAMs because data are usually stored as charge on capacitance which discharges with time. Part of every clock cycle is devoted to this "recharge" process in dynamic RAMs. Dynamic RAMs sometimes have refresh circuitry built onto the chip, and sometimes external refresh circuitry is necessary. RAMs with on-chip refresh circuitry are sometimes called *self-refreshing* or *pseudo-static RAMs.* In either case, the clock frequency is restricted to a minimum value in order to limit the discharge process. Many dynamic RAMs are organized as 1-bit words, which is often an additional disadvantage.

Most semiconductor RAMs are volatile, losing memory when power is removed. However, nonvolatile RAMs are available for applications where high speed is not required. The first nonvolatile RAMs developed were metal nitride oxide semiconductors (MNOS). These devices were discovered accidentally when silicon nitride was evaluated as a metal oxide semiconductor gate dielectric. Unexpectedly, charge became trapped at the silicon dioxide/silicon nitride interface. The charge was retained so well that nonvolatile memories were proposed. Now MNOS memories are used in television tuners, telephone repertory dialers, calculators, and point-of-sale terminals. These devices can be constructed to respond to read times in the range of 1 μs when memory retention requirements are a few days, and can have a memory retention range of years when read times can be extended to approximately 10 μs. Writing is typically a longer process, requiring an erase followed by a write signal on the order of 1 ms. Sometimes these types of memories are called *read-mostly memories* (RMMs).

C. Programmable Read-Only Memories, Erasable PROMs, Electrically Alterable ROMs

Since the programming of a ROM is a relatively major task, more flexible devices are needed for use during system development.

A PROM (*programmable read-only memory*) is a memory device that can be programmed by a user in a relatively short time. The programming requires an instrument called a *PROM programmer.* A typical PROM programmer responds to keyboard input, paper-tape input, or computer input, or can "copy" another PROM. The PROM programmer delivers voltage pulses to the PROM at each location where memory is to be written until, for example, a fusible link has been burned open. This programming is a one-time operation; no erasure is possible.

An EPROM (*erasable PROM*) is a device that can be programmed by electrical inputs that cause charge to be inserted and "trapped" at the programmed location for extremely long periods (possibly years). This trapped charged process is reversible by an intense source of ultraviolet light, which can "erase" the memory (dissipate the trapped charge) over a period of several minutes. These devices are constructed with a quartz window over the memory chip so that ultraviolet energy can be easily transmitted to the memory.

Further flexibility is provided by EAROMs or EEROMs (*electrically alterable* or *electrically erasable ROMs*), which can be written by electrically trapping charge in a manner similar to EPROMs, but which allow selective rewriting of any desired memory locations. The most popular type of EAROM is the FAMOS or *floating-gate device*, which uses two NMOS transistors (one enhancement mode; one with a floating gate) for trapping charge. In a sense EAROMs are similar to nonvolatile RAMs; however, the time involved in altering an EAROM is significantly longer than for nonvolatile RAM.

3.3. SYSTEM ARCHITECTURE

System architecture (putting chips together in an organized structure to form a system) varies considerably depending on the type of microprocessor used. One reason for this variability is that CPU pin connections (connector pins giving electrical access to the CPU) are necessarily limited on microprocessor chips because of small chip size. This pin limitation encourages a variety of approaches to increase system efficiency and allows more pins for peripheral functions such as input/output.

The variety of system architectures is alluded to by the three structures shown in Figures 3.13 through 3.15. Figure 3.13 shows a "conventional" architecture, using a 16-line address bus and an 8-line data bus.

The multiplexed address system shown in Figure 3.14 is used by the 1802 microprocessor to conserve pin connections. At a particular time in the instruction cycle signified by the TPA signal, the most significant address bits are transmitted to a temporary storage device (latch). At the time corresponding to TPB, the 8 least significant address bits are transmitted from the CPU and the most significant address bits are transmitted from the latch so that all 16 address bits arrive simultaneously at the memory.

The F8 microprocessor completely avoids the necessity for address connections to the CPU by not having a PC or an M register on the CPU chip. Instead, these reside in a *static memory interface chip.* Communications between the CPU and the static memory interface chip takes place on the ROMC lines (Figure 3.15). A 16-bit address bus connects the static

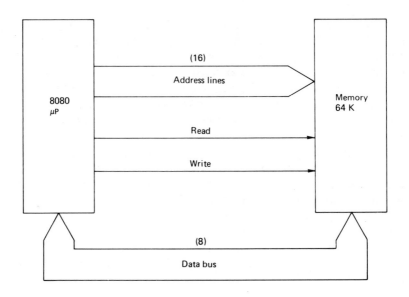

Figure 3.13 Basic 8080 system architecture.

Figure 3.14 Basic 1802 system architecture.

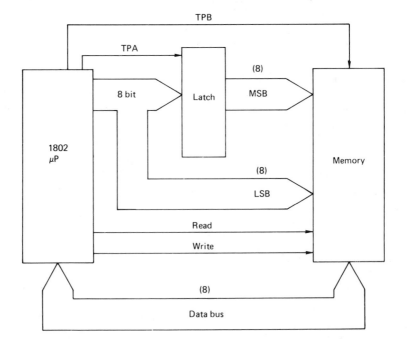

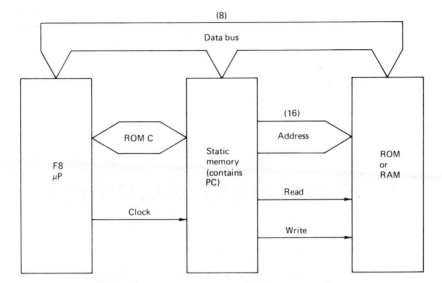

Figure 3.15 Basic F8 system architecture.

memory interface to the memory. In another F8 system architecture, a "program storage unit" is used as a program ROM working in conjunction with the CPU.

BIBLIOGRAPHY

BARNA, ARPAD, AND DAN PORAT, *Introduction to Microcomputers and Microprocessors.* New York: John Wiley & Sons, Inc., 1976.

HILBURN, JOHN, AND PAUL JULICH, *Microcomputers/Microprocessors.* Englewood Cliffs, N.J.: Prentice-Hall, Inc., 1976.

LEVENTHAL, L. A., *Introduction to Microprocessors: Software, Hardware, Programming.* Englewood Cliffs, N.J.: Prentice-Hall, Inc., 1978.

MCGLYNN, DANIEL, *Microprocessors.* New York: John Wiley & Sons, Inc., 1976.

PEATMAN, J. B., *Microcomputer-based Design.* New York: McGraw-Hill Book Company, 1977.

RAO, G. V., *Microprocessors and Microcomputer Systems.* New York: Van Nostrand Reinhold Company, 1978.

VERONIS, A., *Microprocessors: Design and Applications.* Reston, Va.: Publishing Co., Inc., 1978.

WESTER, J. G., AND W. D. SIMPSON, *Software Design for Microprocessors.* Dallas, Tex.: Texas Instruments Learning Center, 1976.

chapter four

Programming Techniques

The efficient use of microprocessors requires a unique blend of hardware and software design talent. The hardware must be selected and organized so that time-consuming transfers, storage, and buffering of data are minimized. The program structure must anticipate hardware using ROM memory (which cannot be written into) and RAM memory (which is usually volatile).

Our previous examination of memory and addressing modes was intended to provide a basis for a more detailed consideration of programming techniques. Efficient programming is often extremely important in the development of microprocessor-based systems. The time required to write programs is usually significant. Volume restrictions often require minimization of memory chips required for program and data storage. The overall system operation speed often depends on how efficiently a control program is written. In this section we will examine techniques commonly used to make programming more efficient.

4.1. LANGUAGE LEVELS

Although a processor operates on the binary digits read from program memory, writing programs in terms of these bit patterns is usually too tedious to consider. Hexadecimal coding of the bit patterns is helpful, but there are other problems. For example, in reading over a program of hexadecimal digits, it is difficult to recognize operations and maintain an overall picture of the program logic. It is also difficult to keep track of location specification. For example, if data and instruction addresses are specified as part of the machine language, and an additional instruction is inserted into the code, the addresses of all subsequent data will be affected. For these reasons, a software aid called *assembly language* is commonly used in microprocessors.[1]

Assembly language uses mnemonic names for instructions, so programs "look like" the operations they are performing. For example, an assembly language program statement might be DCR B for "decrement register B," instead of the hexadecimal code 0D (used in the Intel 8080). Mnemonic names ("memory jogging") can also be assigned to locations, to avoid having to assign specific addresses that might have to be reassigned later. For example, JMP LOOP could indicate an instruction causing the program sequence to "jump" to a location labeled "LOOP." In machine language this same instruction might look like C3621A, where the first byte (C3) is the Op-code for "jump," and the second two bytes (621A) are the address associated with "LOOP."

Before the assembly language program can be executed, it must be translated to machine language by hand or by a software or firmware programming aid called an *assembler*. The assembler translates mnemonic codes into Op-codes and associates the resulting bit patterns with particular memory locations. Then labeled mnemonic addresses are assigned bit patterns representing memory locations. These associations generally require two "passes" through the assembly program by the assembler program. The expense of obtaining an assembler and the time required to run *assembly passes* on an assembly language program is almost always easily offset by the advantages of writing programs in assembly language.

Some computers have resident firmware or software for assembling their own programs. However, for most microprocessors assembly is done on a more powerful processor. Assemblers for one processor that are executed on another processor are called *cross assemblers*.

The use of higher-level languages (FORTRAN, BASIC, PL/M, Pascal, and so on) is becoming more prevalent in microprocessors. These are usually called *compiler languages, interpreters, procedure-oriented languages*, and closely approximate user problems rather than machine execution. For example, a FORTRAN statement such as Y = SQRT (B*B − 4*A*C) would take the place of many assembly language or machine language instructions. However, it must be "compiled" into a machine-oriented language by a firmware or software *compiler* or *cross compiler*. The outputs of compilers and assemblers are called *object codes*. The inputs to compilers and assemblers are called *source codes*.

---

[1]Assembly language is also used in minicomputers and large-scale computers.

An example comparison among compiler language, assembly language, and machine language for a program to move 10 successive pieces of data from one location to another is shown in Figure 4.1.

There are format rules in writing assembly language programs for the convenience of the assembler program. For example, consider the Intel 8080 assembly language statement

LOC:MOV C, M; MOVE MEMORY DATA TO REG C

The colon after LOC signifies that LOC is a label defined by the programmer to represent the address at which the instruction is located (labeling an instruction is necessary only if its location is used in another part of the program). The space between MOV and C separates the Op-code portion of the instruction from the address portion. The comma between C and M separates the register indirect address M from the register direct address C. The semicolon after M signals that the following message is a comment for clarification of the program intended for use by the programmer or anyone else who might read the program. Comments are ignored by the assembler.

Figure 4.1 Example of equivalent programs.

FORTRAN

```
        DO 100 I = 1,10
  100 BLK1(I) = BLK2(I)
```

8080 assembly language

```
        LXI D, BLK1
        LXI H, BLK2
        MVI B, COUNT
  LAB:  MOV A, M
        STAX D
        INX H
        INX D
        DCR B
        JNZ LAB
```

8080 machine language

```
        00010001
        10000000
        00000000
        00100001
        10100000
        00000000
        00000110
        00001010
        01111110
        00010010
        00100011
        00010011
        00000101
        11000010
        00001000
        00000000
```

Special information for use by the assembler is contained in *pseudo-operations*, which are words recognized by the assembler for assigning programs or data to particular portions of memory, marking the start and end of the program or data and defining symbols. Most assemblers also allow the use of symbols to represent a sequence of program steps (macros).

4.2. LOOPS

A large variety of problems require that some action be taken repeatedly so that the same instruction or instructions can be used each time. Some examples are:

1. Processing an array of numbers, for example by adding each number into a sum, or moving a "table" from one part of memory to another.

2. Generating a time delay be executing an instruction of known time duration a prescribed number of times.

3. Executing a convergence routine, where a modified increment is utilized repeatedly until the increment becomes insignificant.

4. Doing high-precision operations on multiword operands, requiring a part of the operand (word) for each instruction execution.[2]

5. Searching an array of numbers for a particular condition (matching a reference number, searching for a maximum value, etc.)

In all these examples, loops are not necessary. The instructions could be written repeatedly. In fact, this would enable the fastest execution time. A loop is utilized to save program instructions and memory space. Usually, programming efficiency and memory space are more important than execution time.

Loops generally have five parts, as shown in Figure 4.2.

1. Initialization instructions setting up pointers, counters, and so on.

2. Execution instructions for performing the main task of the loop.

3. Update instructions to move pointers, increment or decrement counters, and so on.

4. Test instruction to make the decision as to whether to make another pass through the loop or exit.

5. Result instruction to execute the desired task (e.g., storing data) on exiting the loop.

[2]The 64-bit addition problem in Chapter 2 illustrates this type of loop.

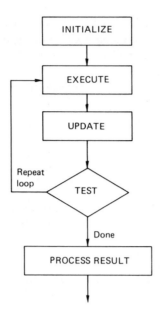

Figure 4.2 Loop program
constituents.

The execution time of a loop is controlled mainly by the execute, update, and test portions.

Loops can be *nested* (loops within loops) to obtain additional power. For example, the nested loops shown in Figure 4.3 represent a program for an 8-bit microprocessor that generates a 1-s delay. A single loop could not conveniently accomplish a delay this great. The delay is obtained by repeated execution of the "decrement B" and "test B" instructions, which take 20 μs.

Since 256 executions are required, escape from the inner loop takes 5.12 ms. Adding 20 μs for decrementing and testing register C yields 5.14 ms for each execution of the outer loop. The initial value of register C is obtained by dividing one second by 5.14 ms, and converting to hexadecimal. The resulting value is C3, which requires 195 decrements to escape the outer loop. This results in a delay of (195) (5.14 $\times$ 10^{-3}) = 1.0s.

Microprocessors have various instructions that specify jumps that can alter the contents of the PC if the test is met. These instructions can be used to create program loops. Examples of tests are: testing the accumulator for "0" (all zero bits), testing the carry flip flop for a "1" (or testing for a zero), testing the accumulator for odd parity (odd number of 1's), and so on.

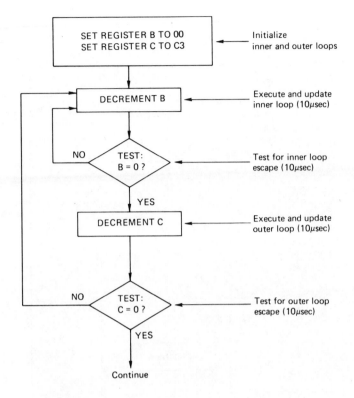

Figure 4.3 One-second delay loop program.

4.3. BRANCHES

Another (more general) way to alter the order of instruction sequence is to *branch*. Branching is based on a test or tests, as outlined in Figure 4.4. Branches can be constructed using instructions that alter the PC based on tests.

An example of a routine that requires a branch is a multiply routine which uses a conditional branch to determine whether the multiplicand should be added as a "partial product" based on testing a multiplier digit. A multiplication routine appears at the end of this chapter.

4.4. STACKS

Stacks are groups of registers or memory locations that are used to systematically store words (usually data) that must be temporarily saved. Words are stored in the stack sequentially and then retrieved in reverse se-

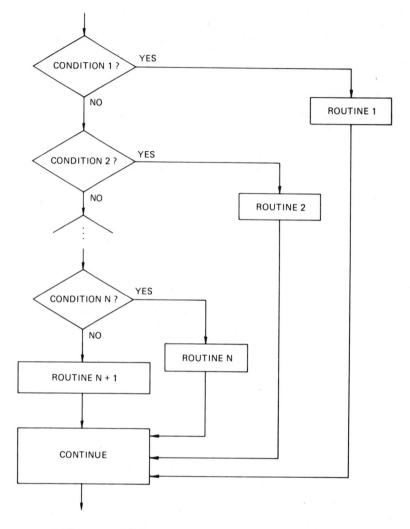

Figure 4.4 General branch routine flow diagram.

quence. This procedure leads to the name *last-in, first-out* memories, or LIFOs. The stack storage process is called *pushing* into the stack; the retrieval process is called *popping* out of the stack.

Most processors have *user-defined* stacks in RAM memory, meaning that the stack location is defined by a processor instruction. Some have CPU stacks consisting of dedicated stack registers.

Processors with user-defined stacks utilize a *stack pointer* (SP) register to specify the stack location. When data are pushed onto the stack, they can be inserted at the address pointed to by the SP, and the SP can be incremented or decremented. When data are read out of the stack, they can be read from the address pointed to by the stack pointer after the stack pointer is changed in the opposite direction.

Figure 4.5 outlines a sequence of setting an SP, followed by pushing two words onto the stack, followed by popping the words off of the stack.

4.5. SUBROUTINES

It is not unusual for a program to use *subprograms* (consisting of a particular set of instructions) repeatedly. If a need for some such *routine* comes up several times during a program, it may be inefficient to program the en-

Figure 4.5 Example stack push–pop routine.

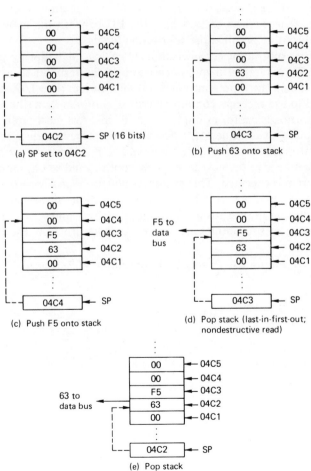

(a) SP set to 04C2

(b) Push 63 onto stack

(c) Push F5 onto stack

(d) Pop stack (last-in-first-out; nondestructive read)

(e) Pop stack

tire subprogram each time. If the subprogram can be "called" into action on demand, it is termed a *subroutine*. The use of subroutines is illustrated in Figure 4.6.

Calling a subroutine requires jumping the PC out of its regular sequence to the memory location where the subroutine begins. When the subroutine is complete, the PC must be *returned* to the main program at a location following the jump. This requires storing the program location information prior to a subroutine call. Some processors do this automatically; some require that the programmer perform the storage. In addition, most subroutines require some sort of data, which vary as a function of subroutine call; in these cases a unique set of data must be made available to the subroutine on each call. Data generated by the subroutine may need to be stored in a particular location prior to each return. The addresses and data that must be conveyed between the program and the subroutine are called *parameters* and the process of tranferring this information is called *passing parameters*. The method of switching the PC between the main program and the subroutine is called the subroutine *linkage*.

Another subroutine consideration is "saving" data during subroutine execution. For example, a microprocessor might respond to an external signal by calling an input/output (I/O) subroutine. The I/O subroutine might need to use registers containing critical program data (the accumulator and status register, for example). Data of this sort must often be saved.

Subroutines can be *nested*, where the main program calls a subroutine, which in turn calls another subroutine, and so on. Return from the innermost subroutine is to the next level of subroutine, and so on, until a return to the program is executed. This process is illustrated in Figure 4.7. Nesting is naturally compatible with LIFO stack operation, since words for the outermost subroutine are pushed onto the stack first, and so on, until words for the innermost subroutines are pushed last. Return from the innermost

Figure 4.6 Example of subroutine utilization.

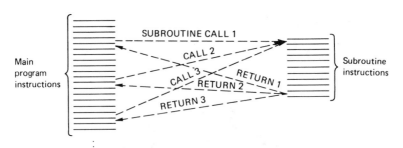

processors, allow user definition of microinstructions through *micropro-gramming*. Microprogrammable microprocessors are generally more flexible, but the increased execution complexity extracts a penalty.

A microprogrammed microprocessor has *microcode* embedded in the processor operation, but it is transparent to the user, who observes only machine language operation.

4.8. PROGRAM EXAMPLES

As an illustration of some of the most basic programming concepts discussed in this chapter, two example routines are listed below, utilizing the mnemonic instruction codes tabulated in Table 2.3.

A. 64-Bit Addition

This problem (binary addition of two 64-bit numbers) was discussed in Chapter 2 and flow-charted in Figure 2.19. The problems associated with using this limited set of instructions are not unlike those faced by microprocessor users in general.

	LD M0 08;	SET MEMORY REGISTER LEAST SIGNIFICANT BYTE TO 08
	LD M1 01;	SET MEMORY REGISTER MOST SIGNIFICANT BYTE TO 01 (M POINTS AT 0108)
	LD R1 00;	SET REGISTER ONE TO 00
	LD R3 08;	SET REGISTER THREE TO 08 (NUMBER OF LOOPS)
	LD A 00;	CLEAR ACCUMULATOR IN PREPARATION FOR CLEARING CARRY FF
	SHL;	SHIFT ZERO INTO CARRY FF FOR CLEAR
LOOP:	LAM;	LOAD ACCUMULATOR WITH DATA POINTED AT BY M REGISTER
	M M0 R4;	SAVE LEAST SIGNIFICANT PART OF M REGISTER IN REGISTER FOUR
	M R1 M0;	MOVE DATA FROM REGISTER ONE TO LEAST SIGNIFICANT PART OF M REGISTER (M NOW POINTS TO OTHER OPERAND)
	ADC;	ADD OPERANDS AND PREVIOUS CARRY
	SAM;	STORE RESULTS IN INDICATED MEMORY LOCATION
	IN R4;	INCREMENT REGISTER FOUR
	M R4 M0;	M0 UPDATED (ONE OPERAND)
	IN R1;	REGISTER ONE UPDATED (OTHER OPERAND)
	DC R3;	REGISTER THREE UPDATED (COUNT)

```
       M R3 A;    MOVE COUNT TO ACCUMULATOR FOR TEST
    JNZ LOOP;     JUMP BACK TO "LOOP" LABEL IF NOT
                  COMPLETE
      LD A 00;    CLEAR ACCUMULATOR IN PREPARATION FOR
                  STORING CARRY
         RSL;     SHIFT CARRY INTO LEAST SIGNIFICANT
                  POSITION OF ACCUMULATOR
    LD M0 08;     SET M REGISTER TO 0108
         SAM;     STORE CARRY IN 0108
         HLT;     HALT
```

B. Multiplication of Two Four-Bit Operands

Assume two 4-bit operands located at addresses 0060 and 0061. Conveniently each has four leading zeros guaranteed so the product will have a maximum of 8 bits of information. The product is to be stored at location 0062, which initially contains 00. The strategy used in the solution is to shift the multiplier right from the accumulator to the carry flip flop in order to successively test each multiplier bit. (A "one" indicates that the multiplicand is to be added into a partial product; a "zero" indicates that it should not be added.) Since each succeeding step in examining the multiplier indicates an additional shift in the relative position between the multiplicand and the partial product (because each succeeding digit represents a higher power of two, which can be accounted for by shifting the relative position), the multiplicand will be shifted left one position as each succeeding multiplier bit is examined. This procedure is demonstrated in Figure 4.9 by an example and a flow chart. This flow chart is then implemented in mnemonic code below.

```
        LD R1 04;   REGISTER ONE INITIALIZED FOR COUNT
START: LD M0 60;    SET MEMORY REGISTER LEAST SIGNIFICANT
                    BYTE TO 60
        LD M1 00;   SET MEMORY REGISTER MOST SIGNIFICANT
                    BYTE TO 00 (M POINTS AT 0060)
           LAM;     MULTIPLIER LOADED INTO ACCUMULATOR
           SHR;     LEAST SIGNIFICANT BIT OF MULTIPLIER
                    SHIFTED INTO CARRY FF
           SAM;     STORE SHIFTED MULTIPLIER BACK IN 0060
        JNC LOC;    JUMP TO "LOC" LABEL IF CARRY = 0
        LD M0 61;   MEMORY REGISTER POINTS AT MULTIPLICAND
           LAM;     MULTIPLICAND LOADED INTO ACCUMULATOR
        LD M0 62;   MEMORY REGISTER POINTS AT PRODUCT
           ADD;     PARTIAL PRODUCT ADDED TO PRODUCT
           SAM;     PRODUCT STORED
  LOC: LD M0 61;    MEMORY REGISTER POINTS AT MULTIPLICAND
           LAM;     MULTIPLICAND LOADED INTO ACCUMULATOR
```

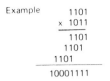

Example
```
    1101
  x 1011
  ------
    1101
   1101
  1101
 ---------
 10001111
```

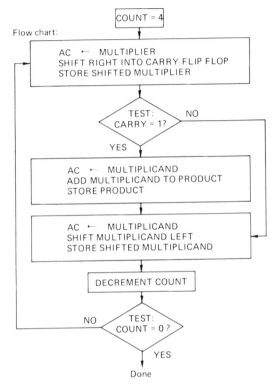

Flow chart:

Figure 4.9 Multiplication routine.

SHL;	MULTIPLICAND SHIFTED LEFT
SAM;	SHIFTED MULTIPLICAND STORED
DC R1;	DECREMENT COUNT REGISTER
M R1 A;	MOVE COUNT TO ACCUMULATOR FOR TEST
JNZ START;	JUMP BACK TO "START" LABEL IF NOT COMPLETE
HLT;	HALT

When compiled, bit patterns would be associated with each Op-code and addresses would be associated with each program step and with labels. However, the mnemonic programs given are indicative of the task a programmer must accomplish.

BIBLIOGRAPHY

BARNA, ARPAD, AND DAN PORAT, *Introduction to Microcomputers and Microprocessors.* New York: John Wiley & Sons, Inc., 1976.

HILBURN, JOHN, AND PAUL JULICH, *Microcomputers/Microprocessors.* Englewood Cliffs, N.J.: Prentice-Hall, Inc., 1976.

LEVENTHAL, L. A., *Introduction to Microprocessors: Software, Hardware, Programming.* Englewood Cliffs, N.J.: Prentice-Hall, Inc., 1978.

MCGLYNN, DANIEL, *Microprocessors.* New York: John Wiley & Sons, Inc., 1976.

PEATMAN, J. B., *Microcomputer-based Design.* New York: McGraw-Hill Book Company, 1977.

RAO, G. V., *Microprocessors and Microcomputer Systems.* New York: Van Nostrand Reinhold, Company, 1978.

VERONIS, A., *Microprocessors: Design and Applications.* Reston, Va.: Reston, Publishing Co., Inc., 1978.

WESTER, J. G., AND W. D. SIMPSON, *Software Design for Microprocessors.* Dallas, Tex.: Texas Instruments Learning Center, 1976.

chapter five

Input/Output

Up to this point we have concentrated on the internal workings of micro-processor-based systems. However, the problems associated with interfacing between the internal system and the outside world are often one of the most complex, expensive, and time-consuming tasks that a microprocessor-based system designer must face. This interfacing is called *input/output* (I/O). I/O is handled in three basic ways, which will be discussed in this section:

1. *Programmed I/O*. This occurs when the CPU takes action to initiate the process through a program instruction.

2. *Interrupt I/O*. The interrupt process is initiated by an external signal asking the CPU for I/O access.

3. *Direct Memory Access (DMA)*. The DMA process is a transfer between the outside world and the microprocessor system memory that takes place independent of the CPU.

5.1. PROGRAMMED I/O

Programmed I/O is fundamentally very similar to transfers from and to memory. I/O devices can be connected to the address, data, and control buses so that they can be addressed by putting a bit pattern on the address bus and can pass data to or from the data bus (see Figure 5.1). The major problems that make I/O more difficult than memory transfers are:

1. *Synchronization.* Inputs to microprocessor-based systems are often controlled by external devices or processors, so that the time an input will occur (or an output be needed) is unpredictable from the viewpoint of the synchronized processing going on in the microprocessor-based system.

2. *Speed.* There are two general classes of I/O devices that cause speed problems: those that are too fast for the microprocessor and those that are too slow. High speed is a problem because of limitations on processing and instruction execution speed; low speed is a problem because it is inefficient for a processor to have to stand idle while waiting on a slow device.

3. *Electrical interfacing.* A microprocessor-based system usually comprises elements from a "family" provided by a particular manufacturer. This eases the electrical interface problems of voltage level matching, current drive capability, and impedance matching. No such matching can generally be expected with I/O devices.

4. *Coding complexity.* Devices that communicate with the microprocessor-based system may speak a different language in terms of how measurement data, characters, commands, and indicator signals are communicated. This requires some code translation.

Figure 5.1 Basic programmed I/O structure.

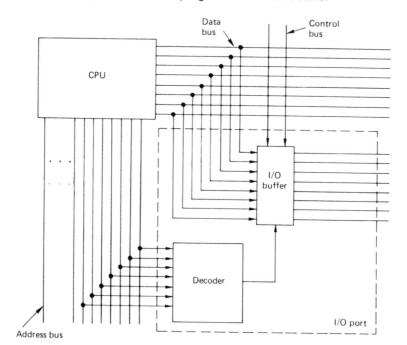

Some example I/O devices are switches, pushbuttons, teletypes, data terminals, floppy disks, cassette tapes, cathode ray tubes (CRTs), analog-to-digital (A/D) and digital-to-analog (D/A) converters, codecs (coder/decoders, typically for interfacing signals like voice), modems (modulator/demodulators, typically for interfacing to transmission devices like telephones), lights, light-emitting diodes (LEDs), motors, solenoids, and so on.

An example of an I/O device especially designed for smooth interfacing is a UART (*universal asynchronous receiver/transmitter*). UARTs are used to interface between the parallel bit requirements of microprocessors and serial external devices. They serve a buffer function and generally have the capability to add check bits of various types. UARTs handle asynchronous external signals and are clocked by the CPU. Similar devices with similar names (USRTs and USARTs) are also used.

I/O paths to the outside world are called *ports.* Ports can be built into the CPU or provided on special devices. For identification, ports have addresses, just like memory locations. In theory, ports can convey any number of bits, but the most desirable number from the viewpoint of the microprocessor is equal to the microprocessor word length.

A device that holds input or output data from the time they become available until the time they are needed is called a *latch.* Although the latching of data is a useful technique, some question remains as to when the data can be unlatched. One way to resolve the question is to establish a two-way communication link.

Handshaking is a technique for establishing two-way communication. Input handshaking consists of providing a *data ready* signal from an I/O port or I/O device to the CPU or I/O interface device associated with the CPU, and an *input acknowledge* signal from the CPU back to the I/O port. When handshaking is used, the CPU will not read data until it receives the data ready signal. The input acknowledge signal allows the I/O port (or device) to unlatch. Output handshaking is similar. It is initiated by a *peripheral request* signal. On recognition of this signal from the I/O device, the CPU sends output data and an *output ready* signal so that the I/O port or device can remove its peripheral request signal and read the output data.

Because I/O operations are usually different from memory operations, I/O addresses are often distinguished from memory addresses. This allows I/O addresses to be restricted to a range that can be described in I/O instructions with fewer bits (8 is a typical number) than are used for memory addresses. However, *memory-mapped* I/O, where I/O and memory addresses are treated alike, is also used. This has the advantage of using common address-decoding circuitry for communicating with memories and I/O ports, and is more efficient in terms of hardware required.

5.2. INTERRUPT I/O

There are many situations where a programmer cannot accurately or efficiently time the need for an input or an output. Some of these are:

1. "Thinking" traffic-light controllers, which do not change state until an automobile arrival is detected.

2. Manual control or override, where the system must respond to a human input when a person decides to initiate an input.

3. Alarm or out-of-limits detection, which is being "awaited" by the system.

4. Asynchronous timing signals from a system the microprocessor must communicate with, but is not locked in synchronism with through a common clock.

In these cases it is attractive to have the capability to recognize an external signal as a call for I/O action. Most microprocessors have this capability, called *interrupt*.

The most common way of incorporating interrupt capability in a microprocessor is to use a microinstruction at the end of each instruction cycle to examine the interrupt input (or inputs). If an interrupt input is detected, the microprocessor suspends its normal operation, "services" the interrupt(s), and "acknowledges" each interrupt so that it can be removed. The microprocessor services the interrupt by executing a special routine to handle the interrupt data (which has been programmed and inserted in program memory, so that upon interrupt it can be called as a subroutine). (Note that interrupt routines can be interrupted, just as subroutines can be nested.) Since the time an interrupt might occur is unpredictable, the interrupt subroutine must make provision for saving any register contents that might be altered by the interrupt subroutine and be needed on return to the main program.

Three problems can be associated with the interrupt process: (1) more than one interrupt request can be received at the same time; (2) more interrupts can be required than the number of interrupt inputs available; and (3) more than one interrupt source requires that some means of identification and priority be formulated.

One commonly used technique for resolving all three of these problems is called *polling*.[1] Polling consists of the CPU or an interrupt-interface

[1]Polling can also be used with programmed I/O.

circuit sequentially examining potential interrupt sources until the active one is found. If more than one interrupt is active, they are serviced in the order that the interrupt sequencer polls them. This order can be varied or remain fixed.

Vectored interrupt capability is available in many microprocessors. The interrupt source puts identifying bits on the data bus during some part of the interrupt process (such as interrupt acknowledge) prior to the time data will go on the data bus. Vectored interrupt capability generally requires more hardware complexity than polling.

Another way to increase capability through the use of hardware is called *daisy chaining*. A daisy chain of interrupt sources is connected by combinational logic, so that the interrupt acknowledge signal is gated past a sequence of sources until an active source blocks it. This allows detection of the first active source in the daisy chain. The identification may be through vectoring. If more than one source is active, servicing succeeding positions in the daisy chain has to await clearing the first active interrupt via the CPU response "acknowledge interrupt." This is illustrated in Figure 5.2.

Some microprocessors have the capability of servicing interrupts on the basis of their importance to the overall process. This is called a *priority interrupt* system. Interrupts can be given priorities by CPU design, by interrupt peripheral device design (e.g., daisy chaining), or by user-added hardware or software. One advantage of software priority is that the priority of a particular input can easily change with time. For example, an input's priority might be increased with time during which it was not serviced to prevent sustained neglect.

Figure 5.2 Illustration of daisy chain logic.

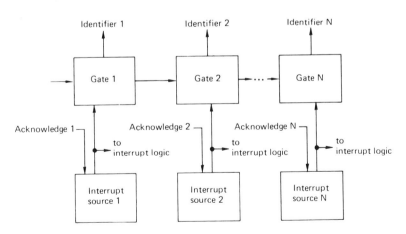

5.3. DIRECT MEMORY ACCESS (DMA)

Very fast memory transfers of large amounts of data are beyond the capability of microprocessor-based systems. However, the problem can be solved by dedicating memory read/write circuitry to the process of moving data at a speed compatible with the memory capabilities. This dedicated process need not be constrained by instruction speed limitations. Most microprocessors have this capability, called *direct memory access*, or DMA.

Since the DMA process requires control of the data, address, and control buses, the CPU can be "idled." It goes to a *wait* state, so that no instruction processes can take place during DMA. This can be initiated by a signal from a *DMA controller* signifying that DMA action is requested. The CPU can complete its current operation and go to an inactive state until it receives a signal from the controller that DMA is complete.

Short DMA processes can sometimes be accomplished during periods when the CPU is not using the buses. This is called DMA *cycle stealing.* During cycle stealing, if DMA is not complete when the CPU needs a bus, the DMA must be discontinued until the next period is available. Periods available for cycle stealing are indicated by a special signal in processors having this capability.

BIBLIOGRAPHY

BARNA, ARPAD, AND DAN PORAT, *Introduction to Microcomputers and Microprocessors.* New York: John Wiley & Sons, Inc., 1976.

HILBURN, JOHN, AND PAUL JULICH, *Microcomputers/Microprocessors.* Englewood Cliffs, N.J.: Prentice-Hall, Inc., 1976.

LEVENTHAL, LANCE, *Introduction to Microprocessors.* Englewood Cliffs, N.J.: Prentice-Hall, Inc., 1978.

McGLYNN, DANIEL, *Microprocessors.* New York: John Wiley & Sons, Inc., 1976.

PEATMAN, JOHN, *Microcomputer-Based Design.* New York: McGraw-Hill Book Company, 1977.

RAO, V., *Microprocessors and Microcomputer Systems*, New York: Van Nostrand Reinhold, Company, 1978.

VERONIS, A., *Microprocessors: Design and Applications,* Reston, Va.: Reston Publishing Co., Inc., 1978.

chapter six

Bit Slice Structure

Bit-slice architecture is available in some microprocessors. This structure allows concatenation of n-bit CPU submodules (n usually equals 2 or 4) to obtain a word length of a multiple of n. For example, if four bit-slice chips of 4 bits each were connected, a 16-bit microprocessor capability would be obtained. Each submodule contains part of the registers and part of the ALU. The resulting processor must be microprogrammed by the user in order to generate usable instructions. A master control unit is used to coordinate the system activity. A block diagram of an example general structure is shown in Figure 6.1.

In this figure, bit-slice devices consist of ALUs and some registers, sometimes called *register-arithmetic logic units*, or RALUs. The microinstructions are generated by the user and stored in microprogram memory, and the machine language instructions are stored in main memory. There is a master control unit.

Bit-slice architecture has the advantage of flexible word lengths and instruction sets. Users can customize programming capability to accomplish desired functions and to optimize speed. Bit-slice processors often offer higher-speed technologies also, since they are not as constrained by size considerations as are ordinary microprocessors. Bit-slice architecture imposes penalties in terms of chips required and hardware/software support necessary. More user skill is required for efficient application.

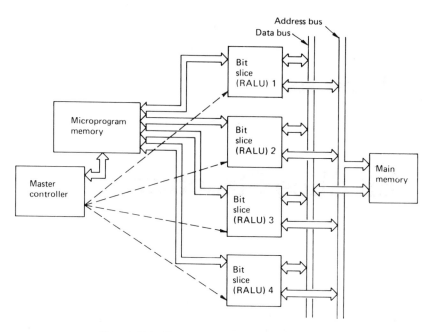

Figure 6.1 Example bit-slice architecture.

6.1. ARCHITECTURE DETAILS

The structure shown in Figure 6.1 has four sections of interest:

1. Microprogram Memory This section contains *microinstructions* (a microprogram) for implementing each processor action. These actions, generated by control signals, are, for example, to transfer data from one register to another, to shift the contents of a register, to latch output results, to add (with or without carry), and to make decisions. A microinstruction contains bits for controlling operations and sometimes bits to signify the location of the next instruction. Each control bit can be dedicated to a specific control signal (nonencoded bits), or control signals can be decoded from bit patterns (encoded bits). Each microinstruction can be accomplished in a single clock cycle (monophase programming); or in multiple clock cycles possibly using overlapped instructions (polyphase programming).

2. Main Memory The main memory contains machine language instructions (*macroinstructions*) similar to those used in conventional microprocessors. However, each corresponds in general to several microinstructions. The correspondence is established by the designer (microinstruction programmer) according to the design rules of the bit-slice processor. The word length is also under the control of the designer. The main memory words can represent instructions or data.

3. Master Controller This section contains the microprogram sequencer. The sequencer controls the flow of machine language instructions from the main memory under control of the microprogram. Each time the microprogram has completed execution of a macroinstruction, a new main memory address is determined (by incrementing the PC or as a result of the previous macroinstruction), and a new macroinstruction is fetched to the IR. The sequencer then decodes the macroinstruction bits, deriving the desired microinstructions, which are executed. The controller can be customized to a particular word length or it can be "bit-sliced" by having small-bit-sized controllers intended for concatenation. Controllers may also contain a push/pop stack to facilitate subroutine execution.

4. Processor The processor comprises concatenated bit-slice devices. Each (RALU) typically has registers, an accumulator, an ALU, and status flags. The aggregate of the bit-slice processors is an overall processor containing full-word-size registers, an accumulator, an ALU, and status flags.

6.2. APPLICATIONS FOR BIT-SLICE MICROPROCESSORS

Bit-slice microprocessors are usually applied where speed requirements, needs for special instructions, or word-length requirements cannot be met with ordinary microprocessors.

Processing speed is enhanced in bit-slice microprocessors because of two main factors. First, since the bit-slice concept requires multiple chips, it is not usually judged very important to pack components densely on chips. This means that high-speed technologies (see Chapter 9) such as ECL and Schottky TTL can be used, whereas the dense MOS technologies usually used for microprocessors are restricted to relatively slow speeds. A second factor is instruction efficiency. Microinstructions can be customized to a particular application. Therefore, the inefficiency due to structured program statements using a fixed number of clock cycles and due to a restricted instruction set is not necessary.

Some applications that typically match bit-slice microprocessor capabilities are: real-time signal processing, such as digital filtering and fast Fourier transforms; process control with heavy real-time data processing requirements; data communication coding, sorting, and transformation; disk controllers; and graphic displays.

6.3. SYSTEM SUPPORT

Microprocessor-based systems require unusual support when compared to conventional systems (see Chapter 9). The hardware structure requires special training, the software development requires particular personnel talents, and the tests necessary require special laboratory equipment.

Bit-slice microprocessors have even more stringent requirements. The system structure is much more complicated, the programming is more difficult because it must be created at a lower (microinstruction) level, and the laboratory equipment required is more complex. The problem is made significantly more severe by a relative lack of support in all three areas. Instructions and guidance for forming system structure are not readily available for bit-slice microprocessors. Software aids such as cross assemblers are not prevalent and are more difficult to use. Laboratory equipment is not generally tailored toward bit-slice processors.

6.4. SUMMARY OF TRADE-OFFS

The use of bit-slice microprocessors depends on evaluating trade-offs involving the advantages and disadvantages of the technique. These are summarized below.

A. Advantages

1. *High speed.* The speed of performing system functions using bit-slice processors is unrivaled by conventional processors for many applications.

2. *Instruction flexibility.* The ability to customize instructions to a particular application or to a family of applications is often extremely powerful.

3. *Tailored word lengths.* Expandable systems can be matched closely to almost any application.

B. Disadvantages

1. *Complex hardware design.* The system structure is necessarily complicated.

2. *Relatively difficult software design.* Programming must be carried out at a more complicated level (microprogramming) than for conventional microprocessors. In addition, macroinstructions must be created.

3. *Limited system support.* Hardware design information, software aids, and laboratory equipment are not generally easily available or applicable to bit-slice microprocessors.

4. *Functional reliability.* The large number of chips and interconnections in a typical bit-slice microprocessor system is detrimental to system reliability.

BIBLIOGRAPHY

ADAMS, W. T., AND SCOTT M. SMITH, "How Bit Slice Families Compare: Part 2, Sizing Up the Microcontrollers," *Electronics*, August 17, 1978.

NIKITAS, A. A., "Bit Sliced Microprocessor Architecture," *Computer*, June 1978.

chapter seven

Design Examples of Intermediate Complexity

The material in preceding chapters was intended to give an overview suffi-cient for understanding a much larger class of problems, such as those to be addressed in this chapter. In order to enlarge one's perception of the types of problems that are amenable to microprocessor-based system implementa-tion, we will first consider these "intermediate-level problems."

7.1. HAND GRENADE GAME

Game Description This game uses an eight-LED display (which represents the "battlefield") and an input button. The battlefield consists of a "ground" or "end zone" on each end of the display (bits 0 and 7) and "air" in between (bits 1 through 6). The grenade position is represented by a lighted LED and moves across the battlefield at the rate of one increment per $\frac{1}{10}$ s. The fuzing time for the grenade is randomly chosen to be 8, 10, 12, or 14 s (representing a grenade from one of four manufacturers) and the starting location of the grenade (initial end zone position) is randomly determined. When the grenade is located in a player's end zone, he or she has the option to hold it or to throw it out. To throw the grenade, the player must press the input button. When the grenade explodes, the processor will determine the losing player and will light all four LEDs on his or her side of the battlefield.

Playing Instructions After loading in the machine code, the game is started by pressing the input button. This will cause a grenade to appear in one end zone or the other (the fuze time is also determined). The game begins as soon as the key is released. As soon as the starting location of the grenade is revealed, the fuze countdown to grenade "explosion" starts. The object of the game is to try to guess the "life" of the grenade and throw it so that the opponent will not have sufficient time to get the grenade out of his or her side of the battlefield before it explodes. At a velocity of 0.1 s/position, the minimum time on one side is 0.7 s. The program is written so that a player throwing the grenade must release the key before the grenade reaches the opponent's end zone. When the grenade "explodes," the processor will signal the loser by lighting all four LEDs on that player's side of the field.

Explanation of the Grenade Program   After startup, the processor enters a counting loop and remains there until the input button is pressed. Then the processor stores the value of a counter (a random number) and waits for the key to be released. When the key is released, the processor uses this random number to determine the initial grenade position and the fuzing time. For this game, 1 bit of binary information is needed to determine which end the grenade will start in, and 2 bits to determine which of the four possible fuze times will be used. Since only 3 bits of the random number are needed, the most significant 5 bits are stripped off by "anding" the number with 07 (hexadecimal, or hex). The least significant bit is used to determine the starting location; thus, by executing a shift right and testing the carry flip flop, the initial starting location and a direction flag are established. The starting address of a table which contains the required constants for the four possible fuze times (the remaining 2 bits) is added. The appropriate constant will then be retrieved from the table and loaded into the timer (see Figure 7.1).

As the processor enters the main timing loop, it first checks to see if the grenade is in either end zone. If the grenade is located in an end zone, that player has the options of holding or throwing it. If he or she chooses to hold it (the button is not depressed), the processor will bypass the shift routine and output the same pattern again (the grenade stays in the end zone). However, if the player decides to throw it, the processor will complement the direction flag (which will cause the shift routine to send the grenade to the other end zone) and proceed to the shift routine. If the grenade is not located in an end zone, the processor tests the direction flag (Direc) and sends the grenade in the appropriate direction, stores it, and displays it. Next a 100-ms Delay routine is executed; then the timer is decremented. If the timer is not equal to zero, the processor begins executing the loop again. If it is zero, thus signaling the explosion of the grenade, the processor will determine the loser by testing the final position on the battlefield of the grenade. All four LEDs are lighted on the side of the losing player, which signals the end of the game.

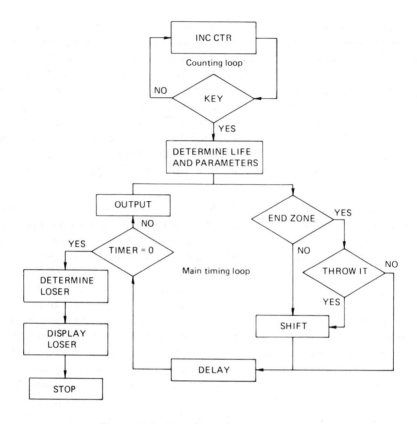

Figure 7.1 Overview of grenade game.

An overview of this program is presented in Figure 7.1. A detailed flow diagram is presented in Figure 7.2.

7.2. SHOOTING GALLERY GAME

Game Description This game uses an eight-LED display as a "shooting gallery" and an eight-button input keyboard as a "gun." The program randomly displays a bird for the player to shoot at (simulated by a lighted LED). The player has 750 ms from the time the bird is displayed to press the corresponding key on the keyboard. If the correct key is pressed, the processor will indicate a hit by momentarily flashing all the LEDs on and off. If the "shot" misses, the bird will be displayed for the remainder of the time, which may allow the player another shot. A game consists of 25 birds or 20 shots (whichever occurs first). At the end of the game, the processor displays the player's score via a hexadecimal output display. A perfect score is 14 hex or 20 birds.

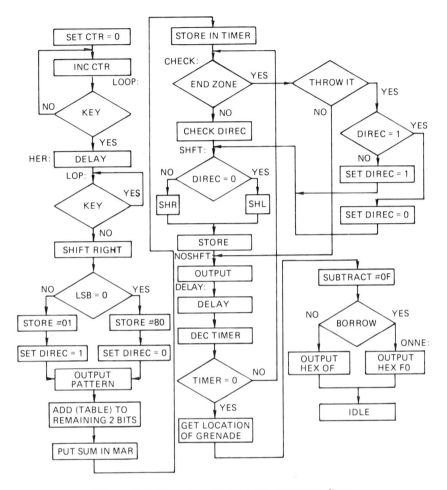

Figure 7.2 Overview of grenade program flow.

Playing Instructions The game is started by pressing any button which causes the first bird to be displayed. The birds are displayed for 750 ms, and then the display is blank for 750 ms. Key 0 "shoots" at LED bit 0; key 1 "shoots" at LED bit 1; . . . ; key 7 "shoots" at LED bit 7. Since there are more birds than shots allowed, the player can be somewhat selective as to which birds he shoots at. After the last bird or shot, the processor will display the score and then stop.

Explanation of the Shooting Gallery Program After startup, the processor begins to generate 7-bit random numbers. These random numbers (pseudo-random) are generated by a linear feedback technique, where the 2 least significant bits of the shift register are exclusive-OR'd (XOR-ed) and the result is shifted into the most significant bit of the register. A schematic representation is shown in Figure 7.3.

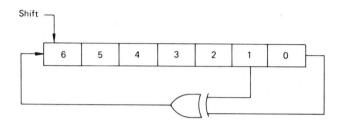

Figure 7.3 Seven-bit shift register.

The generator produces a pseudo-random sequence which repeats every $2^7 - 1$ generations (127 shifts).

The implementation utilizes the accumulator as the shift register and software logic for the exclusive-OR gate. The 2 least significant bits of the accumulator are used to determine the value to be inserted in bit 7. If the exclusive-OR sum of bit 0 and bit 1 is a 1, then bit 7 is set to "1"; if the exclusive-OR is 0, bit 7 is set to "0." The accumulator is then shifted right. A new "random" number is now available in the accumulator in bits 0 through 6. The processor continues in this manner until a key is pressed, which indicates that the player is ready to begin.

The program uses flags to control execution. The first of these is GAME. When GAME is 0, it indicates that the processor has just been started and the player is not ready to begin. Once the game is started, GAME is set to 1, so the random number generator will begin determining the 25 necessary random numbers.

Another flag is DON. When the processor is displaying a bird, DON = 1, and during the blank time between birds, DON = 0 (indicating that the display is blank).

Another flag is KEYFLAG. It starts out equal to 0, but once a key is pressed it is set to 1. KEYFLAG remains 1 until that key is released. This keeps the program from counting a key press as more than one hit or miss. EF3 is a testable input bit which is actuated by the pressing of any key.

To determine the location of the bird, the processor takes the 3 least significant bits of the random number and does a one-of-eight decode to determine which LED to light. After displaying the bird, the timer starts. Before the processor reads the keyboard, it checks DON (to see if a bird is being displayed) and EF3 (to see if a key has been pressed). If these two conditions are true, a read-keyboard subroutine is called. If not, the processor continues in the loop until the timer = 0. When the timer expires, DON is checked to see if the processor should blank the display or obtain another bird (i.e., get a random number). If the display should be blanked, the processor first decrements "BIRDS" to see if the game is over. If the game is not over, DON is set to 0 and 00 is displayed via the LEDs. Then the processor executes the timing loop again to provide the blank display time period. If the game is over, the processor will output the score and stop.

When the read-keyboard subroutine is called, it checks KEYFLAG. If this flag is 1, it means that this key depression has already been serviced. In this case, the subroutine immediately returns to the calling routine (main program). If KEYFLAG is 0, the processor reads the keyboard and determines which key has been pressed by XOR-ing it with transformation values stored in memory. After transformation of the "input" value into the binary number representing its "labeled" value, the program compares the binary value with the binary location of the bird. If the numbers match, the number of shots remaining is decremented and the score is incremented. If not, the number of shots remaining is decremented and the program returns to the calling routine.

A detailed flow diagram is presented in Figure 7.4.

7.3. ELECTRONIC COMBINATION LOCK

An electronic combination lock provides an interesting example. The combination is to be input using an input button. An LED is to be used for "feedback" to the user who is inputting the combination. The user inputs a three-digit combination by successive key depressions in three 4-s time periods. These time periods are indicated to the user by the lock (processor) by blinking the LED ON–OFF–ON (4s in each state). Thus, if the combination is 3, 1, 6, the user would depress the key three times during the first 4-s LED ON Period, one time during the OFF period, and six times during the second ON period. The code is stored in memory. In the case of a valid combination entry, the lock is unlocked. In the case of a bad combination entry, a "bad-combination-message" is output to the user. It is required that the combination input process take the same length of time (12 s) regardless of whether the correct combination is entered or not. Thus, the user receives no indication of where any error was made. The lock is to return to its initial combination entry mode after processing either a good or a bad combination.

Although many methods could be employed to solve this problem, one solution is presented here. First timing diagrams and an overview of the processor timing loop are presented to describe the lock operation from both the user's and the processor's point of view. Next, a brief explanation of the program accompanied by a detailed flow chart (Figure 7.5) is presented.

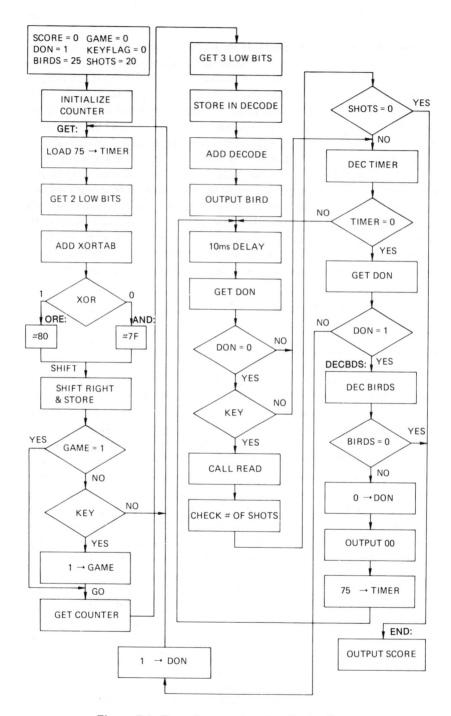

Figure 7.4 Flow diagram for shooting gallery.

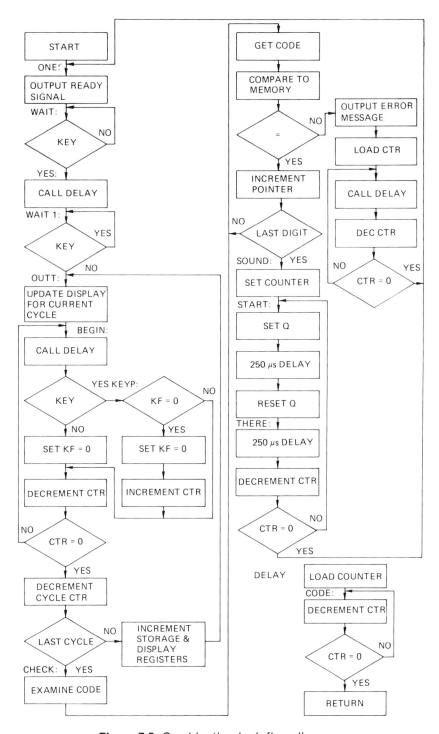

Figure 7.5 Combination lock flow diagram.

A. Timing and State Definition for the Combination Lock Problem

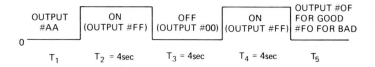

T$_1$ This is the time when the processor is executing a waiting loop searching for a key press. The length of this cycle depends on the frequency of lock use.

T$_2$ After a key press and release, the processor enters T$_2$ and turns on the light on the display. This cycle lasts for 4s. During this cycle the processor inputs the number of key depressions that corresponds to the first digit of the combination.

T$_3$ After the 4s of T$_2$ elapse, the processor automatically enters T$_3$, which also lasts for 4s. During this cycle the processor inputs the number of key depressions that corresponds to the second digit of the combination.

T$_4$ After the 4s of T$_3$ elapse, the processor automatically enters T$_4$, which also lasts for 4s. During this cycle the processor inputs the number of key depressions that corresponds to the third digit of the combination.

T$_5$ This represents the time when the processor checks the entered combination to see if it is correct and then outputs either the error message (#FO) or "opens the door" (#OF), depending on whether the combination was correct or not.

. For the lock program, a main timing loop of 10 ms is employed. A cycle time of 4s requires execution of this loop 400 times.

B. Explanation of Combination Lock Problem

After initial power up, the processor outputs its ready signal (#AA in Hex) and loops while waiting for a key to be pressed and released. A depressed key is indicated by EF3 going to one. After the key has been released, the processor enters the main timing loop. First it outputs the appropriate cycle indicator via the display (T$_2$ = FF, T$_3$ = 00, T$_4$ = FF), and then it begins a 4-s delay. If the key has been pressed, the processor goes to the debounce routine; if not, it decrements the loop counter and executes the loop again. It continues in this manner until the loop has been executed 400 times. If a key has been pressed, the program debounces the key with a software routine. The first time that the processor detects a key press, it sets KF = 1 and increments the appropriate combination counter. The processor will then bypass this counter until the KF is set to zero by key release. Thus, the minimum time between key depressions is equal to twice the loop time, or 20 ms. This procedure provides sufficient debounce time for the input button. During the execution of a cycle, the number of pulses entered is stored in a memory location which is assigned to that particular cycle of the combination. After all three digits have been input, the processor then enters a routine that compares the entered code to the combination which is stored in memory. If the processor finds an error, it outputs an error message (#FO in Hex) and then returns to the ready mode. If the code is correct, the processor will then release the door lock. For this example, #OF is output to simulate opening the door. After unlocking the door for approximately 4 s, the processor returns to the ready mode.

chapter eight

Applications

It is fascinating to survey some of the plethora of commercial products to which microprocessors have been applied. This survey is necessarily limited, because of the incredible variety of products where microprocessors can be efficiently used. However, by considering the applications mentioned, some insight is obtained into how microprocessor technology can improve the performance of information-processing systems.

8.1. GENERAL-PURPOSE COMPUTERS

One of the most obvious applications for microprocessors is in microcomputers. A microcomputer system typically has a microprocessor CPU and peripheral chips, some kind of mass storage (floppy disk, standard disk, cassette tape, or standard magnetic tape) for software and data, a keyboard or terminal, a printer or CRT display for output, and a software system (compiler, assembler, loader, etc.). The first microcomputer was the MITS ALTAIR 8800, designed around the INTEL 8080 microprocessor by an Albuquerque, New Mexico, company in 1974. MITS projected a total market of 200 to 300. They sold that many in one afternoon early in their sales history. Some other examples of microcomputers are PCC ALTAIR 8800a and 680b, PET2001, COMPAL 80, IMSAI, SOL 20, and Altos ACS 8000-6.

Microcomputers differ from minicomputers and large-scale (mainframe) computers in several generic ways, although specific examples may require fuzzy categorizing. A large-scale computer is typically room-size, a minicomputer is racksized (or smaller), and a microcomputer sits on a desk and is easily portable. The price of a large-scale computer may run into the millions of dollars; a minicomputer, tens of thousands of dollars; and a microcomputer, thousands of dollars. Other differences include service and general support, processing speed, memory capacity, and word length, with the microcomputer looking generally less powerful in all categories.

Microcomputers are used in much the same way as large-scale computers or minicomputers, but on smaller scales of price, capability, and speed. Mathematical computations (*number crunching*) can be performed on a number of microcomputers. Many business-oriented functions have been performed with the aid of microcomputers. These include accounting (where arithmetic operation sophistication is minimal, but sorting, tabulating, and memory capabilities are necessary), inventory control (where entry and recall from memory categories is important), and payroll (where accuracy of compiling information and computation is essential).

Microcomputers can also be efficiently applied to many routine business functions, such as address label generation and printing, typing form letters, and generating legal documents. Other applications are sorting and searching tabulations such as real estate listings, stock market analysis, and personnel record keeping.

8.2. PERSONAL COMPUTERS

Recently, *personal computers* based on microprocessors have been available within the price range of a large number of individual consumers ($500 to $1,000); over 200,000 were sold last year. Some of these are the Heath Company H8 (based on an 8080) and H11 (based on an LSI 11), Apple Computer's Apple II (based on a 6502), the Commodore PET, Videobrain Computer's Video Brain (F8), Intelligent Systems' Compucolor II, the Radio Shack TRS 80 (Z80), the RCA VIP (1802), the Three Rivers Computer Corporation PERQ, and the Bally Library Computer (Z80). Generally, the main difference between a microcomputer and a personal computer is that the latter is not intended to provide a tax write-off business expense.

Although some users adapt personal computers to the business applications mentioned above, there are many uses for personal computers that are strictly for personal benefit. The ability to perform logic and generate displays on CRTs makes games a natural application. Standard "library" game software can be purchased, or users can generate their own games. Personal computers can also be used as calculators. Although this might be judged "overkill" in some cases, there are instances where standard calculator precision or capability is insufficient, and personal computers can be programmed to give a satisfactory solution. Personal computers can also be used to store recipes, telephone numbers, check balances, and other records and data. Other applications for personal computers are home learning centers where self-teaching courses are applied, news or information displays where news transmitted by tape or television is linked into the personal computer, and control of household items such as lights, television, sprinklers, and fire extinguishers.

8.3. CONSUMER PRODUCTS

A large number of commercial products use microprocessors. In most, the microprocessor is not apparent to the consumer or user, but nevertheless a substantial benefit in cost or capability is enjoyed. One of the earliest and most obvious applications was in television games such as "Pong," "ATARI," and "Star Wars." The manipulation of objects such as a "ball" and "paddles" is naturally amenable to microprocessor logic. The speed required to generate TV displays is not compatible directly with microprocessor instruction speeds, but DMA capability allows the display to be driven from memory somewhat independent of the processor, except for changes that are generated by the processor for a small percentage of the memory. Other examples of microprocessor-based games include chess (complete with display messages such as: "I expected that!" and synthesized sound messages), checkers, backgammon, basketball, baseball, war (Intercept, Electronic Battleship, Code Name: Sector), and electronic pinball machines.

Dedicated microprocessors have also been applied for several years to calculators and digital watches. Sound synthesis has been applied to both. Microwave ovens have used microprocessors to accept commands for controlling defrost and cooking start and stop and to link these to a display time of day. Washing machines, dryers, sewing machines, cameras, television sets, and turntables are other consumer products that use microprocessors to get improved performance. One of the newest applications is video cassette recorders (VCRs), which use microprocessors in a variety of ways to give better performance (fast and slow motion, stills, preset program selection, commercial editing, etc.).

Commercial electronic laboratory equipment, such as digital voltmeters, computing oscilloscopes, pulse generators, frequency synthesizers, and spectrum analyzers, have begun using microprocessors for automatic ranging, calibration, computation, and function control. PROM programmers use microprocessors to evaluate feedback from the memory that is being altered to determine the proper energy deposition required to properly "burn in" the memory data. Microprocessors are also used in "point-of-sale terminals" to give immediate updating on prices, cash on hand, and item inventory as transactions take place. Scales can use microprocessors to compute prices for weighed items as identification for the item is entered, based on stored data. Card-sense readers and Universal Product code (UPC) readers have used microprocessors.

Electronic funds transfer (EFT) systems that are being initiated in preliminary form are microprocessor users. One example is that of the "automated teller" systems being used by some banks. Cryptographic coding and decoding has utilized microprocessors.

Educators are finding microprocessor-based teaching systems useful in a variety of ways. Simple examples are the addition–subtraction–multiplication–division problem-posing devices such as the "Little Professor" and spelling-word-giving machines such as "Speak and Spell." The spectrum of microprocessor-based teaching aids extends to much more complicated devices (personal computers are used in some classrooms). The Dallas Independent School District is using TRS 80s in its elementary education program. Language translators based on microprocessors are now available for translating words and phrases and for aiding in teaching languages. One product uses sound synthesis for pronunciation.

Communications systems are becoming extensive microprocessor users because of the "distributed intelligence" necessary to implement packet transmission systems, message coding and decoding systems, and error-correcting coding and decoding systems.

"Intelligent terminals" (terminals that can do some form of data handling, such as display control, editing, sorting, or coding) were made possible largely through the use of microprocessors. "Automatic" cartoon movie generation systems have been implemented with the aid of microprocessors to relieve artists from the tedious task of recreating each frame of the movie, incorporating only relatively small changes.

Burglar alarm systems,[1] coded garage door openers, TV tuners, automatic light-control systems, and electronic combination locks are other applications in which microprocessors have been used. The list of items given is necessarily incomplete. New applications appear almost daily.

8.4. MEASUREMENT AND CONTROL SYSTEMS

The last few years have seen extensive microprocessor applications in measurement and control systems. Service station gasoline pumps are becoming extensive users of microprocessors to compute delivery quantities and price and to drive displays at the pump and inside the station. Traffic-light-control systems are becoming more sophisticated through the use of microprocessors. Automobile manufacturers are increasingly turning to

---

[1] The 1978 WESCON microprocessor application award went to a home security system that is now being marketed.

microprocessors for ignition-timing control, carburetion control, anti-skid control, speed control (cruise control), and display of routine and computed information (time, trip mileage, miles per gallon, etc.).

Another interesting application of microprocessors is in tester control. As electronic equipment sophistication increases, so does the complexity of required testing. In order to run an extensive series of tests in a reasonable time, some kind of processor control is necessary. Microprocessor control is beginning to replace minicomputer control in these applications. An example is the Bell System Multi-Button Electronic Telephone tester, developed around a microprocessor by Western Electric. The Multi-Button Electronic Telephone has from five to 40 "pickup" buttons, each corresponding to a line, plus a 10-button direct station signaling array for intercom or paging. The telephone contains an electronic controller which operates on binary data. The amplitude and duration of binary pulses and a variety of message formats and operation sequences must be tested for. Although production quantities are low, a microprocessor-based test system was judged appropriate.

Microprocessors have been used in general aviation guidance computers, industrial time-delay relays, satellite communication systems, and oil-rig-control systems.

In response to the demand for more sophisticated computer systems, microprocessors are beginning to be used as peripheral-control devices, coordinating the flow of information from tape deck and disk memories.

Measurement of eye refraction has recently been automated by microprocessor control in the Dioptron device, which detects reflection patterns from the retina. Range meter accuracy has been improved by averaging multiple measurements under microprocessor control. A distributed microprocessor system has been constructed for weather analysis using data from widely dispersed sources. Microprocessors are naturally attractive for assembly line and industrial control processes (weighing and batching, machining control, parts sorting).

8.5.   MECHANIZATION OF ROUTINE TASKS

Some kinds of analyses lend themselves nicely to microprocessor capabilities if the proper inputs can be provided, such as blood analysis, chromatographs, spectrum analysis, psychoanalysis, and personality analysis. Speech recognition and pattern recognition are difficult for any type of automatic system, but microprocessors have been used in simple applications of this type.

Some attempts have been made at robot design based on microprocessor control. These have ranged from the IEEE "Great Electronic Mouse Race" contest for robots that could solve a maze, to robot mail carts and "household servants" (automatic sweepers). Lear-Siegler has an automated mail cart delivery system that uses a microprocessor. An automatic feeding system for people with paralyzed upper limbs has been developed around a microprocessor.

BIBLIOGRAPHY

Applying Microprocessors. Electronics Magazine Book Series. New York: McGraw-Hill Book Company, 1978.

"Best Bits: Applications of Microprocessors," *IEEE Spectrum*, September 1978.

CANNING, R. C., AND BARBARA McNURLIN, "Micros Invade the Business World," *Datamation*, August 1978.

JURGEN, R. K., "For Detroit: Smaller and Smarter Chips," *IEEE Spectrum*, November 1978.

LEVENTHAL, L. A., *Introduction to Microprocessors.* Englewood Cliffs, N.J.: Prentice-Hall, Inc., 1978.

MENNIE, DON, "Personal Computers for the Entrepreneur," *IEEE Spectrum*, September 1978.

PEATMAN, J. B., *Microcomputer-based Design.* New York: McGraw-Hill Book Company, 1977.

RAMEY, R. L., J. H. AYLOR, AND R. D. WILLIAMS, "Microcomputer-aided Eating for the Severely Handicapped," *Computer*, January 1979.

ROBINSON, A. L., "Microcomputers: The Great Electronic Mouse Race," *Science*, September 1978.

SHANKLAND, T. A., "Microprocessor-controlled Testing of Electronic Telephone Set," *Western Electric Engineer*, October 1978.

"Will Video-Text Systems Travel Well?" Editorial, *Electronics*, September 14, 1978.

chapter nine

The Selection Process

9.1. ADVANTAGES AND DISADVANTAGES OF MICROPROCESSOR-BASED DESIGN

In previous chapters we emphasized information on how microprocessors work and how they can be applied. The question of whether or not to use microprocessor technology is of interest generally and will be explored in more depth in this section.

A. Advantages

One of the biggest advantages of microprocessor-based design is flexibility. A standard system consisting of a CPU, ROM, RAM, and I/O can often be adapted relatively quickly to changes in specifications or to entirely new functions by changing the program in ROM. Risk is minimized, because the new program can be tested by inserting it in PROM for operational checks before ordering a mass-programmed ROM. ROM turnaround time is relatively short, since the memory data are inserted into ROM by the manufacturer as one of the last steps in processing. This ability to make minor (or sometimes major) functional changes without restructuring the entire system is important to designers.

Another advantage is design ease. Many applications lend themselves more naturally to a step-by-step problem solution that can be programmed, as opposed to ordinary sequential logic design procedures (identifying system "states," applying state-minimization procedures, etc.). Microprocessor-based designs usually proceed faster than standard sequential logic designs. This is because of the relative speed with which problems can be programmed and the simplified system interconnections that need to be defined.

Another advantage of microprocessors is that they are produced by a manufacturer as a standard product. Systems of equal complexity can be realized with custom LSI; however, the number of devices produced for a custom application is necessarily small, and all of the design and processing setup that goes into the preparation for manufacture must be amortized over the small production run. Although microprocessors are not the only "standard products" that can be considered (gates, flip flops, SSI, MSI circuits are possibilities), they are the only standard products capable of handling relatively complex functions at a reasonable cost.

Commercial support is another benefit of using a standard product. This support typically takes the forms of second-source availability, manufacturer consultation, definitive literature, support hardware (and software), guarantees for future parts deliveries, and so on.

Another advantage of microprocessors is the ease with which functional simulations can be made. This is because it is easier to simulate the behavior of software performance on computer systems than it is to accurately determine hardware performance. Some of the reasons for this involve subtle timing problems (race conditions in signal propagations through different paths, for example) and temperature effects. Microprocessor designers face the same problems in developing their product, but a buyer is usually spared facing them again, or at least has them minimized. Relatively simple computer simulations used during the microprocessor design phase are generally trustworthy.

B. Disadvantages

Microprocessors are not the best choice for every application. The disadvantages associated with their use should be considered carefully.

One disadvantage of microprocessors is that they require software talent. The traditional logic and circuit design functions necessary to realize digital systems must be supplemented significantly in the software area. This can be accomplished by training hardware people in software usage, or by blending software and hardware people into a team. Both approaches take considerable effort to achieve design efficiency. Although the ability to write software can be learned relatively rapidly, efficient software design for complex problems is not as straightforward. It might be possible to save several ROM and RAM chips by effective software design, so that the hardware package could be strongly influenced by the software. For these reasons, training hardware designers to be software experts is not an easy solution. Blending hardware and software people is also difficult. Many problems require an extensive understanding of both disciplines. This need for interaction can be met by cooperative efforts, but experience shows that the best designs are by people who have a good understanding of hardware and software.

Speed is a disadvantage. Processor-based operations generally require so much structure in their operation that execution efficiency is sacrificed. Also, microprocessor technology is aimed so extensively at small size that higher-speed technologies which require more volume are seldom used.

Another disadvantage of microprocessors is the attendant requirement for support equipment. It is much more efficient to implement a system with the aid of data terminals, cross assemblers, development systems, PROM programmers, microprocessor analyzers, and emulators (which simulate a microprocessor's instruction executions by software executed on some other processor). These items are not necessary in standard design projects. In fact, microprocessor-based design can be accomplished without using auxiliary equipment. However, efficiency is improved dramatically by its use.

Custom LSI is more efficient than microprocessors in utilization of chip area, since no extra capability need be incorporated in the design. Microprocessors almost always have unused capabilities.

Microprocessors also constrain geometry to some extent, because chip sizes and chip packaging are determined by the manufacturer.

C. Trade-offs

At least two considerations are somewhat ambiguous in listing advantages and disadvantages—cost and size.

The cost of microprocessor implementation can be extremely low because high-volume production makes individual chips inexpensive. This advantage would be ameliorated somewhat if custom LSI could be used in large quantities. However, the microprocessor cost is often insignificant compared to the amortized cost of laboratory equipment, software training, and computer charges. Since these might well make microprocessor implementation more expensive, the cost question warrants careful consideration.

Size can often be reduced by the use of microprocessors, since they use LSI technology. However, this also should be examined more closely. For example, the Intel 8080 microprocessor requires a minimum of five or six chips to implement relatively simple functions. One-chip systems are available, but these usually have limited memory capacity. It is apparent that custom LSI usually has at least the potential for achieving smaller designs than microprocessors.

For these reasons, size and cost considerations interact in determining whether microprocessor implementation is advantageous or disadvantageous.

9.2. LABORATORY EQUIPMENT CHOICES

Some of the choices available for laboratory equipment are described in this section.

A. PROM Programmers

PROM programmers are instruments that are designed to insert operator-specified data into a PROM, usually so that the PROM can be used in system development testing. PROMs are purchased with all memory locations in the same state (usually all "ones"), and the PROM programmer selectively (under manual or automatic control) writes "zeros" in the specified locations. PROMs usually must be carefully "programmed" (voltage, current, pulse length, or number of pulses must be carefully controlled). This process requires special capabilities, which PROM programmers provide. PROM programmers usually have other features, such as the ability to copy (totally or partly) from one PROM onto another. Many have "personality cards," so that they can program a variety of PROM types.

B. Data Terminals

Data terminals allow human interaction with most microprocessor systems in order to enter and read out data and programs. They can also be used to communicate with computer time-share networks to utilize cross assemblers or cross compilers, and often have cassette tape storage for programs and data.

C. Logic Analyzers

The complexity of LSI devices, especially microprocessors, has influenced the development of an impressive new family of insruments for easing the troubleshooting headaches that inevitably arise.

A logic analyzer is usually keyed to synchronize on data of interest in microprocessor-based systems, such as bit patterns of data or addresses. The synchronization allows the user to look forward or backward from the synchronization point.

Logic analyzers are available with one or both of two basic functions:

1. *Timing monitors.* Analyzers with timing-monitor capability sample the digital waveforms on the buses, and store and display the data on a CRT as multichannel waveforms. These analyzers are effective for examining hardware operation.

2. *State monitors.* Analyzers with state-monitor capability sample the bus state during each processor cycle, store these data, and numerically or alphanumerically display the data on a CRT as digital state or mnemonic instruction information. These analyzers are effective for finding software "bugs" (errors).

Many analyzers can operate in either mode; however, care should be taken in selecting an analyzer, since it will sometimes be optimized for operation as one or the other type. A number (32 is typical) of high-impedance "probes" are usually available to connect the analyzer to logic devices. Logic analyzers and microprocessor analyzers usually have extensive memory, I/O, and data processing capabilities. They are usually microprocessor-based.

D. Development Kits

Microprocessor developments kits can be purchased from most microprocessor manufacturers to aid in developing a product around their CPU. These systems typically consist of a "prototype system" (microprocessor, ROM, RAM, etc.), I/O control, and a resident loader program.

E. Emulators

In order to be an effective design aid as the prototype development nears its final form, a development system should have an emulator, which is sometimes called an *in-circuit emulator* (ICE). The emulator allows the development system to interface directly to custom prototype hardware by replacing the CPU of the prototype. Emulators typically have additional features, such as "debugging" capability, to allow program stops at specified locations and single-step operation to investigate detailed system behavior. They may also allow user access to signals inside the CPU that would normally be unavailable to a user.

F. Development Labs

A development lab consists of an array of fairly sophisticated equipment surrounding a prototype of the system under development. This equipment serves two purposes:

1. *To monitor and analyze prototype performance.* A logic analyzer

(in conjunction with utility program), scope, meters, pulse generators, and terminal (or TTY) are used in this phase.

2. *To alter and reload the development program.* Large-scale computer software packages, a PROM programmer, and a data terminal are used in this phase.

An effective development lab has all of the elements mentioned previously in some form (with the possible exception of the PROM programmer). In addition, the development lab has some type of convenient data switch (possibly constructed with simple toggle switches) for interconnecting the various equipment with prototype processor systems. Several vendors (e.g., Texas Instruments and Tektronix) provide a general-purpose, integrated development lab. A development lab is an extremely powerful system, with all the elements previously mentioned (except, of course, the prototype and auxiliary equipment such as oscilloscopes and meters) available in an integrated package. Many designers, however, use labs consisting of equipment custom assembled in a similar manner. Figure 9.1 shows a block diagram of a typical development lab.

9.3. SOFTWARE/FIRMWARE CHOICES

Many aids are available that can be purchased as software or as firmware for easing microprocessor-based system development. Some of these are discussed in this section.

A. Assemblers

The ability to automatically *assemble* programs is crucial to efficient microprocessor-based system development. Assembly can take place in the microprocessor itself if a resident assembler is available, on a minicomputer or large-scale computer using a cross assembler, or on a time-share system (also using a cross assembler).

If assembly is carried out on the microprocessor with a resident assembler, the program can be run immediately following assembly. This minimizes turnaround time when compared to the execution of cross assembly on a different computer. However, time-share systems can sometimes be used to write assembled program object codes directly into microcomputer RAM memory, achieving essentially the same result. Also, resident assemblers are often limited in processing speed compared to cross assemblers, which can extract a time penalty. The initial cost for resident assemblers is high compared to cross-assembly time charges, but it can be amortized over a period of time.

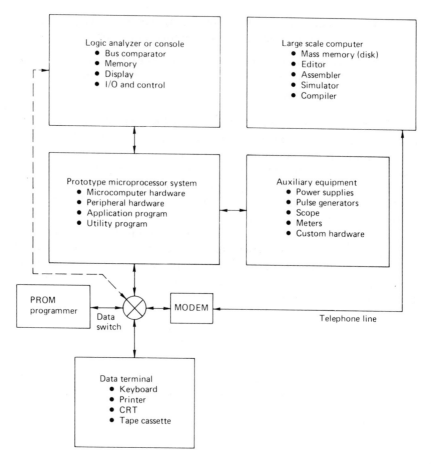

Figure 9.1 Microprocessor development lab block diagram.

B. Compilers

The introduction of *compiler* languages for microprocessors was inevitable. FORTRAN, BASIC, PL/M, MPL, PLZ, and Pascal are examples of compiler (and interpretive) languages that have been applied to microprocessors. These languages are much more powerful than assembly languages because one compiler "statement" can often represent several assembly language program steps.

However, it is not always obvious that compiler capability should be obtained for a microprocessor application. One reason is availability. Compiler languages and compilers are not readily available for all microprocessors. Another reason is cost. In simple controller applications, assembly language programming does not represent a large enough time investment to warrant paying for compiler capability. Also, efficiency is a consideration. Even the best compilers are inherently inefficient when compared to assembly language for some tasks. This is because they predetermine a sequence of machine language steps, representing each compiler language statement without consideration of particular aspects of the task that might allow program reduction.

C. Editors

An *editor* provides the capability to make small changes, additions, and deletions to a source program without retyping the entire program. This may require substantial memory support, since the entire program must be stored for the editor to work on. Editors are especially convenient in refining complex programs where many changes may be necessary during the "debug" phase.

D. Debuggers

A *debug* program uses some sort of "test point" condition to stop program execution at specified instructions (or at offsets before or after specified instructions) so that single-step operation or register dumping (displaying) can begin. This allows the operator to study response at each program step and thereby isolate the machine behavior that is causing a problem.

E. Loaders

A *loader* of some form is essential for getting programs loaded into program memory. For commercial development systems, a loader is typically included in ROM to allow a user to enter data from a keyboard or computer file into sequential RAM memory addresses.

F. Simulators

Simulators are available for many microprocessors in order to test the intended execution of a program through software analysis without actually running it. Typically, simulators are implemented in a high-level language (e.g., FORTRAN) that is executed on a large-scale computer. The simulator program implements all internal CPU operations recognizable to the programmer and provides a simulation of data transfer between the CPU and memory or I/O. This allows testing of microprocessor system software before the hardware is available. Programming errors are easily identified through use of a simulator, but timing problems may not be. Closer imitation of program execution requires a hardware device such as a development system or an emulator.

Figure 9.2 illustrates the integration of many of the software aids mentioned in this section into a software development effort.

9.4. TECHNOLOGY CHOICES

The selection of a microprocessor is often determined by the technology used in fabricating the microprocessor. In this section we will consider the technologies commonly used and the design parameters of interest affected by these technologies.

Figure 9.2 Software development procedure.

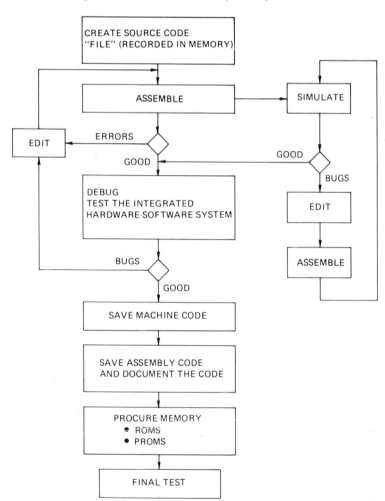

A. Semiconductor Processing

Crystalline semiconductor materials are used to make microprocessors because their electronic properties can be controlled by the selective addition of impurities ("doping") to achieve signal amplification and logic functions.

Typical elemental crystal-lattice semiconductors are diamond, silicon, and germanium. Silicon is almost universally used as a basic material because it is more stable than germanium and has nearly ideal electrical properties. Silicon doped with phosphorus or arsenic contains mobile electrons in its structure, which can transport electrical energy. This is called *n*-type silicon. Silicon doped with boron or aluminum has electron voids (holes) in its structure, which can also transport electrical energy. This is called *p*-type silicon. These two types of silicon are basic to the technologies described in this section.

Transistor-Transistor Logic (TTL) TTL has been a basic technology in SSI and MSI for years. It uses *bipolar transistors* (similar to the type invented by John Bardeen, Walter Brattain, and William Shockley in 1947). Bipolar (junction) transistors amplify signals by using a small current (base current) to control a larger current (emitter-collector current). Both *npn*- and *pnp*-type devices can be created. In *npn* devices, electrons carry the emitter-collector current; in *pnp* devices, holes carry the emitter-collector current. Because of relatively high power dissipation, TTL is difficult to use in LSI circuits. Modifications have been made to TTL to decrease power consumed and increase speed, such as adding a structure called a *Schottky diode* (which prevents saturation) to obtain *Schottky TTL* and *low-power Schottky TTL*. Figures 9.3 and 9.4 show examples of a TTL circuit and a Schottky TTL circuit, respectively.

Emitter-Coupled Logic (ECL) ECL uses bipolar transistors operating in an emitter-follower-like mode that enables rapid charge switching for high speed, but at a penalty in power consumed. This technology has been important in developing high-speed computers and minicomputers, but has been used only in bit-slice microprocessors. Figure 9.5 shows an example of an ECL circuit.

Integrated Injection Logic (I²L) I²L is a relatively new bipolar technology that uses an unusual circuit configuration (current source and multiple-collector transistors) to give high speed, low-power operation. The speed–power interaction is somewhat constrained so that extremely low power operation is possible at low speeds, and high speeds are achievable at the expense of higher power. Figure 9.6 shows an example of an I²L circuit.

Fairchild Semiconductor has obtained some improvement by using I³L (Isoplanar I²L).

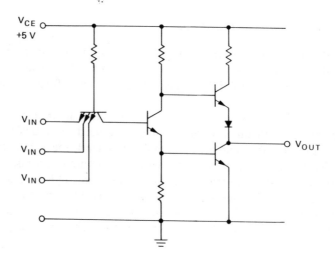

Figure 9.3 Example TTL circuit.

Figure 9.4 Example Schottky TTL circuit.

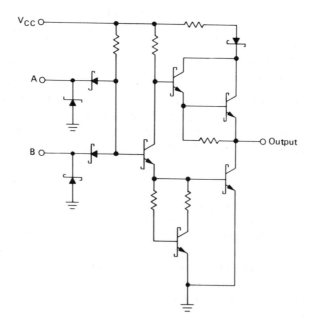

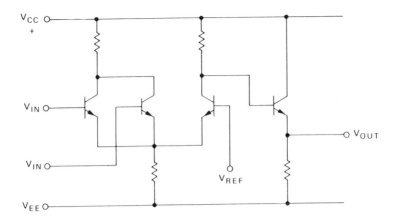

Figure 9.5 Example ECL circuit.

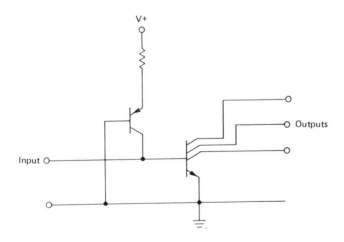

Figure 9.6 Example I²L circuit.

PMOS PMOS devices are part of a family called field effect transistors. Although these devices were conceived long before the invention of bipolar transistors, the fabrication technology did not become practical until the 1960s. MOSFETs are metal-oxide semiconductor field effect transistors which use a deposited metal gate to control charge flow. If the charge is conveyed by holes, the devices are called PMOS. PMOS was the first technology applied to LSI and microprocessors. It is simple, reliable, and well understood. PMOS logic uses resistive loads, either in the form of active PMOS devices or resistors. Figure 9.7 shows an example of a PMOS circuit.

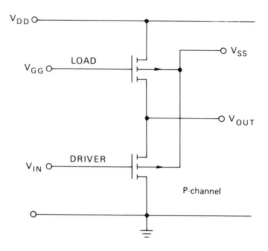

Figure 9.7 Example PMOS circuit.

NMOS   NMOS transistors are MOSFETs that convey charge through electron conduction. Both PMOS and NMOS can be fabricated in high-density configurations and lend themselves readily to LSI. NMOS is more difficult to make than PMOS but yields higher density and higher performance (the electrons give more mobile charge conveyance). NMOS logic uses resistive loads, either in the form of NMOS devices or resistors. Figure 9.8 shows an example of an NMOS circuit. Some improvement in performance has been obtained by etching V-shaped grooves into the silicon surface and taking advantage of the third dimension in the geometry to con-

Figure 9.8 Example NMOS circuit.

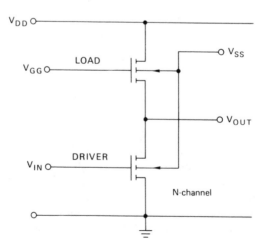

dense the space used for the devices (VMOS). Some other size and performance benefits have been provided by scaled MOS (HMOS, HMOSII, and XMOS).

CMOS   Complementary MOS uses PMOS and NMOS devices in a pair to form a single logic device without a resistive load. The gates of each member of a pair are connected together (cascaded) so that an electrical signal that turns the PMOS device on turns the NMOS device off, and vice versa. The devices are connected in series so that power consumed is minimized, although some power is expended during switching due to circuit capacitances, and during a brief period when both the NMOS and PMOS devices conduct. CMOS devices have been especially popular with digital watch manufacturers because of the low power dissipation. Figure 9.9 shows an example of a CMOS circuit.

Some improvement in device performance can be achieved by using a sapphire substrate on which a thin layer of silicon is placed (silicon on sapphire, or SOS). This structure results in improved isolation and reduced capacitances, thereby improving speed and component density capabilities for comparable device geometries. However, CMOS/SOS requires sophisticated processing and materials technology. Other CMOS improvements have been obtained using P^2C-MOS (double polysilicon) and ISO-C-MOS.

B. Parameters Influenced by Technology

It is interesting to relate parameters that influence performance of a microprocessor-based system to the technologies available. It is not unusual for this type of consideration to necessitate the choice of a particular technology.

Figure 9.9 Example CMOS circuit.

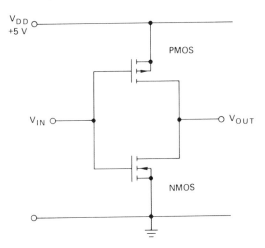

Speed   The rate at which a microprocessor clock can run and its instruction execution rate depend strongly on the speed with which a signal can propagate through a gate ("gate delay" or "switching time"). The actual operation speed of a microprocessor depends on instruction efficiency and chip layout efficiency as well as speed of gate response, but gate delay is a useful measure of the speed capability of a technology. The highest-speed technology used in microprocessors is generally considered to be ECL; PMOS is the slowest. Figure 9.10 displays the relative position in the speed spectrum of other technologies by plotting gate delay. Because of the variety of manufacturers and techniques, the values shown are approximate.

Density   The density with which components can be structured on a chip influences how much capability can be designed into a microprocessor. Density is influenced by the geometry required, the power dissipated, and the interactions between adjacent devices. A common measure of density is gates per unit area. I^2L and NMOS probably have the greatest capability for density; TTL requires the most chip area. The density spectrum for other technologies is shown in Figure 9.10.

Power   Power consumption is often important in system performance, especially if operation powered by a small battery is required. CMOS and SOS offer distinct advantages; ECL in contrast requires a relatively large power source. Power consumption per gate is plotted in Figure 9.10 for a variety of technologies.

Environmental Hardness   There are many applications, especially in military systems work, for devices that must withstand extreme environments such as radiation and temperature extremes. In these cases environmental hardness is important. In general, CMOS/SOS is probably the best technology for environmental hardness, with CMOS and ECL being second. NMOS is the worst. However, CMOS/SOS presently has unproven reliability and may never be competitive (in this regard) with bulk technologies.

One measure of hardness is shown in Figure 9.10. This is the rate of application of γ radiation ($\dot{\gamma}$) that typically causes logic upset (changing a stored 0 to a 1, or vice versa) in memory circuits.

Cost   Cost is not usually considered a very important parameter because semiconductor chips are generally of almost insignificant cost when compared to the rest of a microprocessor-based system. However, the cost of microprocessors could be important if a high-volume production run with a small profit margin is involved. A useful measure of cost is cost per gate and this is shown in Figure 9.10. PMOS is the least expensive technology and ECL is the most expensive.

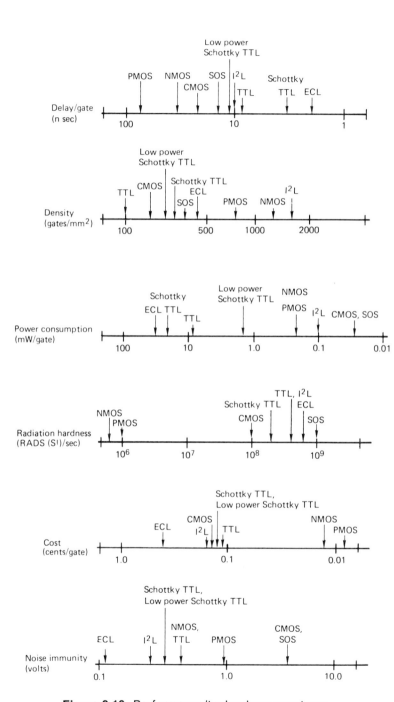

Figure 9.10 Performance/technology spectrum.

Noise Immunity Noise immunity is often important because it determines whether a microprocessor-based system can operate, for example, on aircraft power, in the vicinity of electric motors, or in the presence of an electromagnetic environment (EMR or EMP). It is also related to the tolerance required on power supply voltages, and therefore might determine whether or not regulated power supplies must be used. A measure of noise immunity is the approximate voltage variation that must be applied to a gate input to change the "state" of a logic memory device (change a stored 0 to a 1, or vice versa). This is plotted in Figure 9.10 (CMOS and SOS have the best noise immunity; ECL the worst).

Miscellaneous Other considerations that can enter into the microprocessor selection process are:

1. *TTL compatibility.* TTL has been such a widely used technology in logic circuits that a microprocessor-based system might have to interface with TTL. TTL-compatible microprocessors are advantageous in these situations because they do not require special level-matching and impedance-matching circuitry.

2. *Product use history.* There are arguments favoring selection of a mature technology, since many unexpected problems usually arise in early technology development. Other advantages are that an accumulation of useful user information becomes available and viable second sources are more likely.

3. *Existing laboratory support equipment.* Once an investment has been made in extensive hardware and software support for a particular microprocessor, future selection may be strongly influenced.

4. *Designer preference.* A designer who favors a particular technology or microprocessor may need no other reason than personal reference for making a selection.

9.5. MANUFACTURER AND MODEL CHOICES

The question of selecting a particular microprocessor as the CPU for a microprocessor-based system depends on several factors, to be discussed in this section. At the end of the section are tabulated (Table 9.1) a representative list of currently available microprocessors, along with pertinent information on each.

A. Performance Parameters

The performance parameters of a microprocessor are measures of how well it will do its job. Some of these can be deduced from the technology used in the microprocessor fabrication, as discussed in Section 9.4. However, the evaluation of a particular technology is seldom sufficient. For example, the clock speed is a measure of how fast execution can take place, but variations in microprogram structures between microprocessors sometimes make this at best a coarse measure. Manufacturers' data on instruction execution time are also helpful, but variations in instruction efficiency are also common.

For these reasons, *benchmark programs* are often used to assess microprocessors. The benchmark program is a simple routine written to accomplish some simple function of a type that looks useful in a particular application. Two parameters easily obtained from a benchmark program are the time required to complete the program, and the words of program memory required for storing the program.

Several data points obtained from three example benchmark programs are shown in Figure 9.11. These are similar to fundamental routines that are commonly used. The multiprecision decimal-add routine adds two numbers, each containing 16 decimal digits, represented by a BCD code (binary-coded decimal) consisting of 64 bits. The interrupt routine recognizes an interrupt, saves the accumulator and status register data, and then restores it. The data movement routine moves 100 words of data from one memory area to another. All the microprocessors shown are assumed to be operating at their maximum frequency.

B. Architecture

We have already seen that microprocessor architectures are dissimilar. One architecture might be more suited to handling a particular problem than another. For example, the Motorola 6800 has two accumulators, which is advantageous in handling computations. The RCA 1802 has a reasonably large scratch pad memory, which allows deleting a RAM requirement in some applications. The Fairchild F8 has an on-chip timer, which saves considerable software in some timing routines. Architecture diagrams are available from microprocessor manufacturers.

C. Instruction Power

The instruction set is also an important consideration. A microprocessor with an efficient instruction set might save considerable time for the programmer, has the potential to execute routines faster, and may reduce the amount of program memory (and thereby ROM chips) required. For example, some data processing applications require multiplication. Some microprocessors have a multiply instruction in their instruction set; some do not. The instruction set can be evaluated by studying instruction lists available from microprocessor manufacturers.

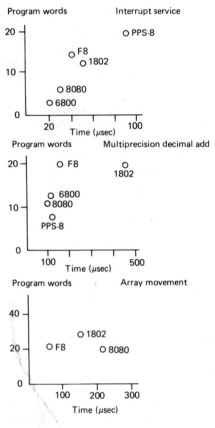

Figure 9.11 Example benchmark programs. The data for the interrupt service routine and the multiprecision decimal add routine were obtained from J. B. Peatman, *Microcomputer-based Design* (New York: McGraw-Hill Book Company, 1977).

D. *Word Length*

Since a variety of word lengths are available, this parameter could be important in choosing a microprocessor. If extensive high-precision data processing is required, a 16-bit microprocessor might be the best choice, but a 4-bit microprocessor might be chosen for a simple controller application. Decimal digits are often represented by a BCD code, so that 4-bit microprocessors are often used in calculator applications. Handling ASCII (an eight-digit code for a set of characters, including the alphabet) information suggests an 8-bit capability. A/D converters commonly make 12 bits available.

E. Number of Chips Required

In applications where size is important or chip count must be minimized for other reasons, it is important to evaluate the number of chips required to realize a system. For example, the popular Intel 8080 microprocessor requires five to seven chips for the simplest applications, whereas the Fairchild F8 CPU and ROM pair might accomplish the same task. During the past two years, a significant number of microprocessors have been announced that have ROM and RAM on the CPU chip so that single-chip systems are possible.

F. Cost

The price of the chips that must be purchased is usually important only if large production runs or low profit margins are strong considerations. However, the overall cost of securing hardware and software support equipment, and indirect costs such as salaries required to support hardware and software design personnel, are often important and can be a function of the microprocessor selected.

G. Support

Another important consideration is the support that can be obtained in the form of hardware (e.g., development systems) and software (e.g., assemblers). It is not unusual for a relatively new microprocessor to be weakly supplied in these areas. It is also useful if the manufacturer has a large selection of associated chips available, such as peripheral interface chips, interrupt logic circuits, and DMA controllers.

It is sometimes important to select a manufacturer with strong indications of stability, particularly if a long production run utilizing the manufacturer's product is anticipated. Some indications available involve past history, corporate financial resources, and availability of an extensive device family, including ROMs, RAMs, PROMs, and interface circuits. The availability of second sources is also comforting. Parts availability and delivery time are also important.

These considerations are emphasized because of the number of microprocessors that have been withdrawn from manufacture and the number of microprocessor manufacturers that have gone out of business or at least out of the microprocessor business.

H. Miscellaneous Considerations

Other factors that should be noted because of their occasional importance include interrupt capability and priority structures, number of I/O ports available, and capability for microprogramming (microprogrammability).

Table 9.1

REPRESENTATIVE MICROPROCESSOR LIST*

Microprocessor	Manufacturer	Bits	Technology	Approx. Cost ($)	Approx. Voltages (V)	Approx. Maximum Clock (MHz)	Comments
MC14500B	Motorola	1	CMOS	3.75	3–18	1	Four dedicated 1-bit I/O lines
MN1498, -99, 1599	Panasonic	4	NMOS	—	5	1	—
MCS-40 family (4004, 4040)	Intel	4	PMOS	6	15	0.750	12-bit addresses
PPS-4/1	Rockwell	4	PMOS	3–18	5, -17, -12	0.200	—
T3472	Toshiba	4	NMOS	13	5	1	12-bit addresses; micro-programmable
TMS1000 family	Texas Instruments	4	CMOS, PMOS	2	3–15	1	On-chip ROM, RAM; currently highest volume microprocessor
S2000, 2150	American Microsystems	4	NMOS	3	9	1	On-chip ROM, RAM
COP 400 family	National Semiconductor	4	NMOS	7.50	4.5-9.5	1	Most models have on-chip ROM, RAM
COP 420, 421	National Semiconductor	4	CMOS	—	2.4-6.3	0.250	On-chip ROM, RAM
HMC S45	Hitachi	4	PMOS	9	-10	0.750	On-chip ROM, RAM
CDP 1802	RCA	8	CMOS	7-16	4-12	6	First 8-bit CMOS processor commercially available
3850 (F8)	Fairchild	8	NMOS	9	5, 12	2	Minimum two-chip system
MCS-80 (8080A)	Intel	8	NMOS	8	5, -5, 12	3	Most popular microprocessor

*These data (and the market in general) are dynamic.

MCS-85 (8085A, 8085A-2)	Intel	8	NMOS	15	5	3	Improved version of 8080A
MCS 650X, 651X	MOS Technology	8	NMOS	8	5	4	Powerful addressing modes
MC6800	Motorola	8	NMOS	9	5	2	Uses two accumulators
MC6802	Motorola	8	NMOS	12	5	4	On-chip stack
MC6803	Motorola	8	NMOS	—	5	3.5	16-bit counter/timer
MC6809, 6809E	Motorola	8	NMOS	—	5	2	Two accumulators can be used as 16-bit AC
SC/MP II (8060), 8070/72	National	8	NMOS	10	5	4	12-bit addresses; NMOS version of PMOS SC/MP
PPS-8, PPS-8/2	Rockwell	8	PMOS	20	5, −17, −12	0.250	Extensive (109) instruction set; on-chip ROM, RAM
2650A, A-1, B, B-1	Signetics	8	NMOS	13	5	2	On-chip stack, indexed addressing
Z80	Zilog	8	NMOS	10	5	4.5	Improved version of 8080A
8008, 8008-1	Intel	8	PMOS	25	5,−9	0.800	14-bit addresses
LP8000	General Instruments	8	PMOS	10	5,−12	0.800	Series 8000 chip set has 24 I/O lines
8085AC	RCA	8	CMOS/SOS	—	5	5	CMOS version of 8085
CDP 1804, 1804C	RCA	8	CMOS/SOS	—	5–10	8	On-chip ROM, RAM
PIC 1645, -50, -55, -70	General Instruments	8	NMOS	3	5	1	On-chip ROM, RAM
MCS-48 family (8048, 8748, etc.)	Intel	8	NMOS	15–90	5	6	On-chip ROM, RAM
87C41, -48; 80C48	Intersil	8	CMOS	—	5–10	6	On-chip ROM, RAM
MK3870, -72, -73, -74, -76	Mostek	8	NMOS	6–10	5	4	On-chip ROM, RAM (except -74)
MC6801	Motorola	8	NMOS	50	5	3.5	On-chip ROM, RAM

Table 9.1 (continued)

Microprocessor	Manufacturer	Bits	Technology	Approx. Cost ($)	Approx. Voltages (V)	Approx. Maximum Clock (MHz)	Comments
146805	Motorola	8	CMOS	—	5	3.5	On-chip ROM, RAM
R6500/1	Rockwell	8	NMOS	9	5	2	On-chip ROM, RAM
Z8	Zilog	8	NMOS	10–15	5	8	On-chip ROM, RAM
INS8040, -50, -60, -70, -72	National	8	NMOS	—	5	10	-50 has on-chip RAM, ROM
IM6100	Intersil	12	CMOS	10	5,10	8	Emulates DEC PDP-8 minicomputer
T3190	Toshiba	12	PMOS, NMOS	47	5,-5	2	Microprogrammable
8088	Intel	16 (8-bit external bus)	NMOS	78	5	5	Comparable to 8086 except for external bus
9440	Fairchild	16	I²L	75–160	5, 1	12	Isoplanar I²L, emulates Nova minicomputer ("Microflame I")
9445	Fairchild	16	I²L	250	5	20	"Microflame II"
mN601	Data General	16	NMOS	56	5, 10, 14, -4.25	8	Micro Nova emulator
CP1600, 1610	General Instruments	16	NMOS	30	5, 12, -3	5	Power interrupt structure
MCS-86 (8086)	Intel	16	NMOS	87	5	5-8	1M-byte addressing, uses two asynchronous processors
MC68000	Motorola	16	NMOS	250	5	8	32-bit ALU and internal registers; 16M-byte addresses
Am29116	Advanced Micro Devices	16	ECL	—	5	10	Microprogrammable

8900	National Semiconductor	16	NMOS	48	5, -5, 12	2	NMOS replacement for PACE
NS16008, -16, -32	National Semiconductor	16	NMOS	—	5	—	NS16008 has 8-bit external data bus
TMS9900	Texas Instruments	16	NMOS	31	5, -5, 12	4	Four-phase clock
SBP9900A	Texas Instruments	16	I²L	190	5	3	Single-phase clock
TMS9980A, 9981	Texas Instruments	16	NMOS	16	5, -5, 12	2.5	8-bit data bus
Z8000	Zilog	16	NMOS	107–140	5	4-8	Segmented version addresses 8M bytes, powerful (> 110) instruction set
WD9000	Western Digital	16	NMOS	130	5, -5, 12	3	"Pascal Microengine" directly executes Pascal
TMS 9940	Texas Instruments	16	NMOS	—	5	5	On-chip ROM, RAM
Series 3000	Signetics	2-bit slice	Schottky T²L	9	5	10	Microprogrammable; good I/O
9400 family	Fairchild	4-bit slice	CMOS or Schottky T²L	30–50	5	12	Microprogrammable
SN54/745481	Texas Instruments	4-bit slice	Schottky T²L	13	5	15	Microprogrammable
MC10800	Motorola	4-bit slice	ECL	30	-5, -2	20	Microprogrammable
IMP-16 (00A/520)	National	4-bit slice	PMOS	22	5, -12	5	IMP uses 4-bit slice
Am2901A	Advanced Micro Devices	4-bit slice	Schottky T²L	10	5	15	Microprogrammable
F100220 family	Fairchild	8-bit slice	ECL	—	-5	50	Microprogrammable
2920	Intel	28-bit analog processor	NMOS	250	5, -5	2.5	Analog inputs, digital processing, analog or digital outputs

117

BIBLIOGRAPHY

CAPBELL, ALAN, DARYL KNOBLOCK, LARRY MATHER AND LARRY TOPP, "Process Refinements Bring CMOS on Sapphire into Commercial Use," *Electronics*, May 26, 1977.

CAPECE, R. P., AND N. MOKHOFF, "Semiconductors," *Electronics*, October 26, 1978.

DUGAN, TOM, BOB LUCE, BOB GREEN, AND BOB MORRIL, "XMOS μCs Bring Power Savings, Speed and Programmable Options to Single-Chip Revolution," *Electronic Design* 17, August 16, 1979.

EVANS, D. C., "On the *Intrinsic* Radiation Hardness of Several Microprocessors," Internal Sandia Laboratories Memorandum, November 1979.

HAVON, D. H., *Electronic Materials and Devices*. Boston: Houghton Mifflin Company, 1975.

JENNE, F. B., "Grooves Add New Dimension to V-MOS Structure and Performance," *Electronics*, August 18, 1977.

KING, E. E., "Radiation Effects and LSI Technologies," Naval Research Laboratory Report.

LEVENTHAL, L. A., *Introduction to Microprocessors: Software, Hardware, Programming*. Englewood Cliffs, N.J.: Prentice-Hall, Inc., 1978.

Microelectronics. San Francisco: W. H. Freeman & Company, 1977.

PEATMAN, J. B., *Microcomputer-based design*. New York: McGraw-Hill Book Company, 1977.

SCHINDLER, MAX, "Can One μC Development System Be 200 Times More Powerful Than Another? Shop and See," *Electronic Design* 25, December 6, 1978.

WESTER, J. G., AND W. D. SIMPSON, *Software Design for Microprocessors*. Dallas, Tex.: Texas Instruments Learning Center, 1976.

chapter ten

Project Management Problems

In this chapter problems of special interest to managers will be discussed. These include fiscal data, documentation expectations, test and reliability data, and warnings about possible pitfalls.

10.1. PROJECT COSTS

Although project costs are highly variable, the figures given in this section are reasonable enough to give a feel for the fiscal picture.

Hardware Costs The cost of the microprocessor is usually a very small part of the hardware cost associated with a microprocessor-based system. Memory chips for use during development and in the final product, I/O devices, clock circuitry or crystal control, power supply circuitry, and mechanical parts (printed circuit board, cabling, switches) usually dominate the hardware costs. Some of these costs are tabulated below. Note that the figures given are for commercial-quality items.

Item	*Typical cost (approximate)*
CPU	$10
ROM	$10 each plus $700 mask charge
RAM	50
EPROM	30
Printed circuit board (PCB)	40
Miscellaneous cables, hardware	25

The figures given above assume the use of a microprocessor-based design. The total semiconductor chips cost depends on the overall system complexity. A rough idea of this cost as a function of the application can be obtained from Table 10.1.

Table 10.1

APPROXIMATE SEMICONDUCTOR COSTS

Application	Number of Chips	Approximate Semiconductor Cost
Simple controllers, appliance control	1 or 2	$ 10
Games, instruments	5–10	75
Complex controllers	10–15	200
"Smart" terminals	10–15	300
Dedicated minicomputer	20–30	600

The software design time depends on many variables, including program complexity. It includes activities such as negotiating software performance specifications, modifications to improve performance and incorporate new features, checkout and debugging operations, and testing and documenting (comments, flow charts, written descriptions). Commonly quoted productivity is about 2 to 15 checked-out lines of program per day depending on the job complexity, with an overall average of about 10.

Laboratory Equipment Costs   Laboratory support equipment such as that listed below can influence design efficiency substantially. However, it is mostly expensive and can usually be replaced with other more time-consuming techniques. The amount of cost amortization that can be justified is an important question. Some cost figures are listed below.

Item	Typical Cost (approximate)
Development kit	$200
Logic analyzer	$500–2,000
Microprocessor analyzer	5,000
PROM programmer	2,000
TTY	2,000
Microprocessor development laboratory	$5,000–25,000

Another option is the purchase of an assembled system called a single-board computer (SBC) for approximately $250. This is a unit similar to a development kit, containing a CPU, ROM, RAM, and I/O.

Delivery times are long and getting longer (see Table 10.2).

Table 10.2

APPROXIMATE DELIVERY TIMES

Component	Delivery Time (weeks)
EPROM	10–22
PROM	8–35
Bipolar RAM	7–18
CMOS RAM	10–15
4K dynamic RAM	9–15
16K dynamic RAM	25–35
1K static RAM	1–14
4K static RAM	10–20
Masked MOS ROM	12–20
Microprocessors	8–22

Software Costs   Software support is important, for example to provide an assembly language capability. Software can be purchased, or it can be rented through a time-share system. Typical costs are shown below. Once a software package has been purchased, it can usually be amortized over numerous applications.

Item	Typical Cost (approximate)
Assembler	$1,200
Simulator	700

Time Expended   One of the attractive features of a microprocessor-based system is that design time is often more than cut in half.[1] Development time is usually dominated by system design, where specifications are negotiated and general approaches are agreed upon.

Electrical hardware design is simplified when compared to comparable custom systems. Mechanical hardware design is about equivalent to that of ordinary systems. Software development is an expense unique to processor-based systems. Some approximate times are listed below.

Item	Time Expended (approximate)
System design	Highly variable, but relatively long[2]
Hardware design	Highly variable, but relatively short
Software design	Three worker-months for 1K ROM

[1]This can be reduced even further if a single-board computer (SBC) is used.

[2]As an example, microprocessor CPUs typically take on the order of a year (depending on the amount of commonality with previous units) and memories take on the order of a few months.

10.2. DOCUMENTATION

In microprocessor-based design, ordinary documentation needs to be supplemented by software documentation. This is analogous to hardware documentation and needs to be just as detailed. Software details cannot be totally supplied by a program listing, although a listing is necessary. In addition, extensive comments and flow charts are useful. The flow charts should be broken down into successive levels of complexity, just as are hardware block diagrams. These features are necessary if it is ever required to modify or understand the program, even if the requirement is imposed on the one who originally wrote the program.

10.3. TESTING

Microprocessors, like other semiconductor integrated circuits, are extremely reliable.[3] However, there is an "infant mortality" effect that makes thorough testing essential for high-reliability applications. This is especially necessary because quality may vary from vendor to vendor and even from lot to lot of the same vendor. Testing usually includes electrical testing, thermal cycling, and visual inspection. Microprocessor electrical testing strategies vary. It is a foregone conclusion that the devices are impossible to test completely because of their complex functional capabilities and pin limitations. Some of the approaches that have been used are listed below.

1. Test ability to meet the end function required.

2. Program the microprocessor to give patterned outputs (e.g., all ones, all zeros, alternating ones and zeros).

3. Program algorithms to exercise individual modules or registers in the CPU (e.g., write data into registers; then read data from the registers).

4. Program a variety of selected or random instructions and compare outputs with those from a "standard" microprocessor known to perform correctly.

10.4. PITFALLS

It is useful to consider some of the many things that can go wrong in a microprocessor-based project. Some of the items we will consider are unique to microprocessors; some are not.

---

[3]Failure rates after initial mortality are usually less than about 0.01% per 1,000 hr.

1. *Lack of appropriate laboratory support equipment.* This can seriously affect project efficiency.

2. *Underpowered microprocessors.* It is better to have more capability than needed than to come up short because system specifications need to be changed or because manufacturers' specifications are not met.

3. *Overdependence on manufacturers' specifications and delivery-time quotes.* Although most manufacturers do not intentionally mislead the customer, there is a general tendency toward optimism.

4. *Underestimation of software development time.* Software development time usually increases faster than linearly with program complexity because of interactions between various parts of the program.

5. *Dependence on a particular manufacturer for parts over a long production life.* If the manufacturer stops making the part or goes out of business, the project is jeopardized.

BIBLIOGRAPHY

ARNOLD, W. F., "Equipment Costs Worry Chip Makers," *Electronics*, November 23, 1978.

"Fundamentals of Microcomputer Systems," *Mini-Micro Systems*, November–December 1977.

LYMAN, JERRY, "LSI Boards Give Testers Fits," *Electronics*, November 23, 1978.

"Microprocessor Project Management," *Course Notes*, Course III, Integrated Computer Systems, Inc., Culver City, Calif.

"Semiconductor Lead Times Lengthening," *Aviation Week and Space Technology*, July 2, 1979.

"The Shortage Tune Plays On," *Electronics*, July 5, 1979.

chapter eleven

Prognosis

At the beginning of this book we spent some time looking at technological history in order to portray a background for the work to follow. Another benefit of studying history is that it often gives a good basis for extrapolating into the future. In this chapter we will try to assess the future in a number of areas. However, it is important to realize that prognosticating is always a risky endeavor. The field we are studying is going through rapid changes, and surprises occur at an amazing rate. Also, there may be many areas where "experts" disagree on the prognosis. Nevertheless, it is worthwhile to ponder what may lie ahead.

11.1. PERFORMANCE TRENDS

Word Size   One measure of performance is word size. The obvious trend is upward. The first microprocessors were 4-bit devices, with calculator-like applications in mind. Eight-bit devices quickly followed because of terminal applications. These are by far the most widely used microprocessors today. Some early work was done on 12-bit and 16-bit processors, mostly to provide devices that could use existing minicomputer software. Recently, more 16-bit devices have begun appearing because there are applications (mostly data processing) for handling 16-bit data.[1] There are con-

[1]The three most widely publicized of the new 16-bit microprocessors are the Intel 8086 (1M-byte memory addressing capability, 6-byte instruction queue for pipelining, fetch—execute in parallel); the Zilog Z8000 (8M-byte memory addressing capability in one version, 24 16-bit scratch pad registers, multiply/divide instructions, coded memory access); and the Motorola 68000 (16M-byte memory addressing capability, 16 32-bit registers, multiply/divide instructions).

siderations being given in industry to 32-bit microprocessors. It would not be surprising to see some of these announced within the next year or two. One reason for the increased effort toward larger word sizes is that more computational power is afforded at a very small price differential. This is be cause technological advancements allow more and more complexity to be designed into a chip. Selling the chips in quantity allows amortization of the development costs, and chip manufacturing costs are relatively low as long as device yields remain reasonably high.

A valid question then is: Will small-word-size processors, especially 4-bit, disappear? Contrary to earlier conjecture, the answer apparently is no. Even if extra capability can be obtained at about the same cost, controller applications remain that are better suited to 4-bit processors. For example, for small word sizes, shifting operations do not have to involve strings of unused bit positions. Also, there are fewer pins to interface from the chip to the outside world for small-word-size processors, and the chips are generally smaller. The largest-selling microprocessor, currently, is a 4-bit single-chip device, the TMS1000. Apparently, the spectrum of microprocessor word size will continue to remain fixed at the low end and will continue to expand at the high end (to 32 bits and possibly 64 bits) for several years.

Speed One reason that microprocessors have been identified as relatively slow speed devices is because the semiconductor technologies most amenable to high component densities have been relatively slow. Effort has been expended in several areas to improve this situation, and it seems certain that speed capability will continue to increase. One approach that has been taken is to modify normal processor architecture to take advantage of *pipelining* (assembling data and instructions into a queue so they are immediately available when needed) and/or parallel processing or *multiprocessing*, where more than one task is pursued at the same time. Another approach is to use geometrical modifications to decrease circuit capacitance and to give more dense devices. This generally allows increased speed of operation.

Dramatic changes in technology may not be too far off. For example, gallium arsenide (GaAs) has provided the substrate for high-speed devices used in RF applications and has been used in some MSI devices. It is possible that GaAs can eventually be used for an LSI substrate, which would allow significant speed increases. Other possibilities include garnet substrates, transverse electron devices, Josephson-junction logic, and dielectrically isolated emitter-coupled logic. The combination of work in these areas virtually assures that there will be significant speed increases (possibly order of magnitude) over the next several years.

As an added impetus, the Department of Defense has embarked on a 6-year program to sponsor a $200 million effort in developing high-speed technology. This activity is called the *very high speed integrated circuit* (VHSIC) project. Although the driving motivation is for more efficient satellite communication, there will probably be technology advances that can be applied to improve microprocessor performance.

11.2. EFFICIENCY TRENDS

Improvements are being made continuously that increase efficiency. These include increased component density and decreased cost per gate or cost per memory element.

Component Density   Integrated circuits entered the marketplace in 1960. Improvements have been made continuously since then in many areas, including component density on an integrated circuit. In 1964, Gordon E. Moore, then director of research at Fairchild (now president of Intel), observed that the number of elements on an integrated circuit had doubled every year up to that time. He suggested that this measure of density would continue to double every year into the foreseeable future. Deviation from this predicted trend (called Moore's law) has been slight since then. Although few people expect progress to continue at the past rate for as much as, say, the next 10 years, there seems to be no doubt that improvement will continue to be impressive. Figure 11.1 displays the history of component density. The curve is now showing signs of flattening, partially because density capability has been increasing faster than the applications needs (Figure 11.2).

At present, improvements are being made in lithography (replacing photolithography with electron beam lithography, or using direct electron beam processing, for example) to improve line resolution. Also, geometrical modifications to existing technology (e.g., VMOS) and new technologies (bubble memories, charge-coupled devices) have been introduced.

An example of the surprising obstacles that can occur in the effort to increase density is the *alpha-particle effect*. A few years ago, malfunctions in extremely dense dynamic RAMs were attributed to alpha-particle emission from minute traces of radioactive elements (uranium, thorium) in integrated-circuit packaging materials (gold-plated metal and ceramics). An alpha particle entering the silicon surface causes an electron-hole pair, resulting in an extremely small discharge. If this discharge is a small percentage of the total charge present, no problem results. This was the situation until high-density devices were fabricated that operated on extremely small charges. The problem that has become apparent consists of occasional changes (soft errors) in stored information. Possible remedies include using different geometrical or material techniques to confine larger charge within the memory element volume, refining material impurities to a cleaner state, and using error-correcting code techniques either external to the chip or within the chip to override infrequent errors. Some problems have also been seen in static memories, possibly due to current induced on bit sense lines.

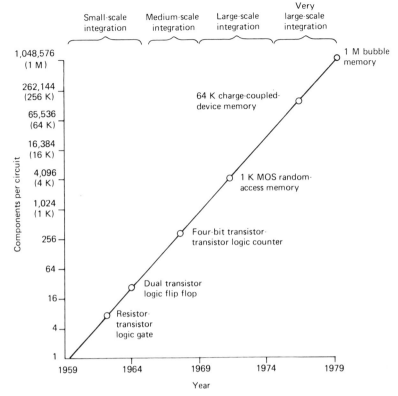

Figure 11.1 Component density trend.

Figure 11.2 Logic and array density trends.

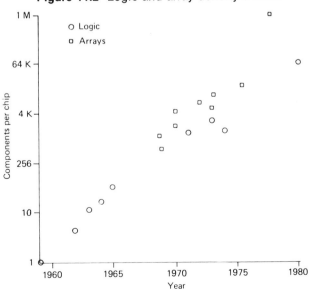

Limited-value polysilicon load resistors have been used to overcome this effect. In spite of the obstacles, continued improvement in component density measures is generally expected for at least several years.

Cost   Cost for semiconductor components generally decreases rapidly in a device's early history because of a learning curve in ironing out technical problems and production details. Also, development costs are usually amortized over early production. One illustration of this phenomenon was the electronic calculator, where consumers who paid about $300 for calculators several years ago can now buy calculators with much more capability for $20. However, after a few years, costs (and prices) stabilize. The overall picture for the consumer continues to get better, however, because of the introduction of new, more efficient devices. An illustration of this phenomenon is shown in Figure 11.3. Here, memory cost per bit is plotted as a function of time for dynamic RAMs through their history, since the introduction of the 1K dynamic RAM in 1973. Expected cost projections are extrapolated into future years. Note that cost per bit is not a completely comprehensive measure of value, since higher-density memory devices generally reduce system volume, lower assembly cost, and give increased performance and reliability. The same technology advancements that improve memory cost per bit provide a basis for more powerful CPUs. Thus, the cost of "processing power" decreases even more rapidly than the cost of memory.

Memory cost is plotted as a function of type of memory in Figure 11.4. Access time is also depicted. Both access time and cost are improving rapidly, especially for MOS RAMs and magnetic bubble memories.

11.3. SOFTWARE TRENDS

It is apparent that dramatic increases in efficiency and decreases in cost are limited to hardware. In fact, software costs continue to increase because programmer salaries are increasing.[2] This imbalance between hardware trends and software trends has been recognized for several years, but only recently has pressure been brought to bear on methods for improving software utilization.

One technique being looked at is called *modular programming*. This is a concept for using program modules for standard tasks in much the same way that logic modules are used for standard circuit functions.

Structured programming is also being examined. A structured program language forces rules on the programmer which make program "bugs" (errors, inconsistencies) less likely. Pascal is an example of a compiler language that is block-structured and is becoming very popular as a high-order microprocessor compiler language. Pascal was first written by

---

[2]This neglects individual efficiency increases due to "learning-curve" effects in new applications.

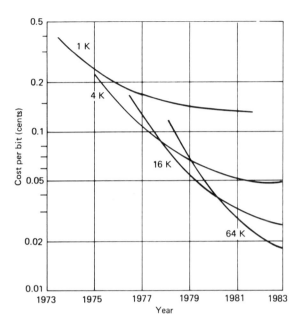

Figure 11.3 Memory cost trends.

Figure 11.4 Memory cost performance.

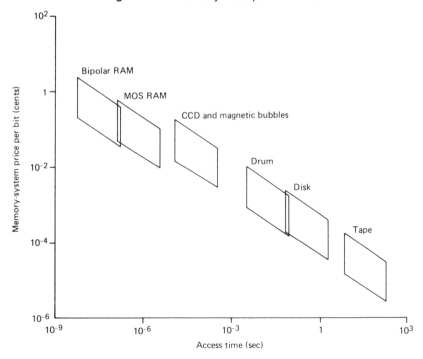

129

Niklaus Wirth in Zurich, Switzerland, in 1968, and has since been applied to most computers ranging from the Cray-1 down to many microprocessors. In Pascal the variables are specified under a program heading, and six sections are used for declaring labels, declaring constants, declaring data formats, declaring variables naming functions, and coding the procedure.

11.4. DOMINANT TECHNOLOGIES

The dominant microprocessor technology has been (and continues to be) NMOS for about the past 5 years. However, it now has competition from SOS, I²L, HMOS (scaled NMOS), XMOS, and VMOS in general attractiveness. Assessment of the future at this particular time is not completely certain; however, it is clear that NMOS will remain the dominant technology for several years.

11.5. MILITARY TRENDS

Military usage of microprocessors has developed rather slowly. The military accounts for 7% of the integrated-circuit sales and 2% of the microprocessor sales in the United States. Part of the explanation is that military usage often demands special processing and capabilities for small-volume applications. Therefore, vendors are unlikely to find the military user an attractive customer. Another factor is that military designers hesitate to go into production with a component they do not know will be available throughout the production run. They are more likely to use microprocessors only in applications where they can "buy ahead" for the entire program. However, the situation is changing rapidly because microprocessors are becoming a better product in military environments and the military pressure on manufacturers is increasing. The 8080A, the Motorola 6800, and the Am2901 are currently military-qualified and others are in process. A safe forecast is that military usage will increase dramatically over the next several years.

11.6. TESTING

Testability of LSI is a difficult problem because the functional capability on a chip is complex, yet there are only a few points of access for the tester. Now with VLSI chips available, testing constraints are being felt strongly. We are fast approaching the time when testing will be the most expensive (and possibly least complete) step in microprocessor production. IBM, Hewlett-Packard, and others have begun allotting a portion (about 5%) of their LSI chips to testability or self-test features.

Some (e.g., Bell Laboratories and IBM) memory chips use redundant lines that can be interrupted by a laser cut so that faults can be tolerated and bypassed. Another remedy (favored by Tektronix) is to use error-correcting codes built into their software on the assumption that the hardware cannot be completely tested. "Signature analysis" data compression of test results is being widely used because of efficiency considerations. It seems certain that there will be considerable effort in testability features in the next few years.

11.7. ARCHITECTURE

When microprocessor technology is pushed to its limits (as it is now in several areas) in terms of speed or efficiency, nonstandard architectures must be considered. Pipelining and distributed processing are already being applied in microprocessors to a limited extent. It seems apparent that the use of architectural techniques similar to this will be increasing for at least several years.

Even memory strategies are being improved. For example, automatic power down (a technique for reducing power significantly between accesses) has been incorporated in some devices.

11.8. SOCIAL IMPACT

It is interesting to consider the effect of microprocessors on society. For example, because of this technology, a calculator or digital watch can be purchased for less than $10. A personal microcomputer can be purchased for less than $600. Estimates are that there are now at least 300,000 personal microcomputers in the hands of hobbyists. The impact of the new processing power available in the home and office and in commercial and business products is awesome to contemplate. Will children forget (or never learn) math? Will all office business be conducted from the home? Will the home be run by robots? The best guess at present seems to be that although someday these events may occur, they are a long way off. The capability to handle complex tasks is available, but personal preference seems to be to the contrary. For example, the teaching process in many kinds of classes could be completely handled by a microprocessor-controlled system. However, most teachers and students seem to prefer an educational atmosphere where they interact with people rather than machines. The same attitude prevails in the business world. Also, much of this impact depends on easily usable prepackaged programs, which are difficult to provide, or increased programming capability among society in general. This is also a slow, difficult process to achieve. It seems unlikely that these types of social impacts will be significant in the near future.

However, the impact of microprocessor capabilities on small businesses is already being felt strongly and will likely become even more important in the future.

Overall, consumer and business products are becoming dramatically more powerful because of microprocessors. There seems little doubt that imaginative designers will continue to generate ingenious applications of microprocessors for the benefit of consumers and businesses.

BIBLIOGRAPHY

ALTMAN, LAWRENCE, "Digital LSI Moving Fast As MOS, Bipolar Processes Speed Up," *Electronic Design 4*, February 15, 1979.

AVERY, G. E., "JJ's: Are They Military Technology?" *Military Electronics/Countermeasures*, September 1979.

CAPECE, R. P., "Alphas Stymie Statics," *Electronics*, March 15, 1979.

CAPECE, R. P., "The Race Heats Up in Fast Static RAM's," *Electronics*, April 26, 1979.

DAVIS, SAM, "Microprocessors" (Special Report), *EDN*, August 5, 1979.

"Fundamentals of Microcomputer Systems," *Mini-Micro Systems*, November–December 1977.

"Get Minicomputer Features at Ten Times the 8080 Speed with 8086," *Electronic Design*, September 27, 1978.

HEFTMAN, GENE, "CMOS-on-SOS Puts New μPs, Memories on the Horizon," *Electronic Design*, November 22, 1978.

HNATEK, E. R., "Semiconductor Memory Update—Part I: ROMs," *Computer Design*, December 1979.

JONES, H. H., AND D. FINCH, "VLSI in Military Applications," *Military Electronics/Countermeasures*, November 1978.

KLINGMAN, E. E., "Comparisons and Trends in Microprocessor Architecture," *Computer Design*, September 1977.

LYMAN, JERRY, "LSI Boards Give Testers Fits," *Electronics*, November 23, 1978.

PHILLIPS, D. H., "GaAs Integrated Circuits for Military/Space Applications," *Military Electronics/Countermeasures*, March 1979.

POSA, J. G., "PASCAL Becomes Software Superstar," *Electronics*, October 12, 1978.

"Powerful Contender Coming for 16-bit μC Designs," *Electronic Design*, July 5, 1978.

Rao, G. R. M., and John Hewkin, "64-K Dynamic RAM Needs Only One 5-Volt Supply to Outstrip 16-K Parts," *Electronics*, September 28, 1978.

Reddy, Rama, "MNOS Devices Remember after the Lights Go Out," *EDN*, August 20, 1978.

"64-K RAM Unveiled by U.S. Chip Maker Outperforms 16-K Units," *Electronics*, September 14, 1978.

"There's a Miracle Chip in Your Future," *Reader's Digest*, October 1978.

Twaddell, William, "Technology Update: Magnetic Bubble Memories," *EDN*, August 20, 1979.

Waller, Larry, "Missile Makers Eagerly Await LSI," *Electronics*, October 12, 1978.

Walsh, Bill, "View from the Top," *Military Electronics/Countermeasures*, August 1978.

Williams, T. W., and K. P. Parker, "Testing Logic Networks and Designing for Testability," *Computer*, October 1979.

chapter twelve

On Keeping Current

Microprocessors are the center of a storm of activity, with daily changes taking place. The only way to keep current in this field is to make a concerted effort. In this chapter, suggestions are presented that might prove helpful in guiding the effort.

12.1 MAGAZINES

There are a large number of magazines that report in detail developments related to microprocessors. Among these are *Electronics, Datamation, Electronic Design, EDN, Kilobaud, Personal Computing, ROM, Interface, Mini-Micro Systems, Computer Design, Byte,* and *Dr. Dobb's Journal of Computer Calisthentics and Orthodontia*. These magazines are news-oriented, as opposed to the more technical literature found in *Proceedings of the IEEE, IEEE Transactions on Electronic Devices*, and so on. One can keep current in the subject matter of this book by reading one or two news-oriented magazines.

12.2. BOOKS

Books on microprocessors are now plentiful. Some are hardware-oriented, some software-oriented, some fairly balanced. Books are not quite as current as magazines, but give better overall perspective to the subject. It is important to make these part of the reading regimen. Some samples are:

Barna, Arpad, and Dan Porat, *Introduction to Microcomputers and Microprocessors.* New York: John Wiley & Sons, Inc., 1976.

Hilburn, John, and Paul Julich, *Microcomputers/Microprocessors.* Englewood Cliffs, N.J.: Prentice-Hall, Inc., 1976.

Leahy, W. F., *Microprocessor Architecture and Programming.* New York: John Wiley & Sons, Inc., 1977.

Leventhal, L. A., *Introduction to Microprocessors.* Englewood Cliffs, N.J.: Prentice-Hall, Inc., 1978.

McGlynn, Daniel, *Microprocessors.* New York: John Wiley & Sons, Inc., 1976.

Osborne, Adam, *An Introduction to Microcomputers,* Vols. 0–3. Osborne and Associates, Inc.

Peatman, J. B., *Microcomputer-based Design.* New York: McGraw-Hill Book Company, 1977.

Rao, G. V., *Microprocessors and Microcomputer Systems.* New York: Van Nostrand Reinhold Company, 1978.

Veronis, A., *Microprocessors: Design and Applications.* Reston, Va.: Reston Publishing Co., Inc., 1978.

12.3. SHORT COURSES

Courses in microprocessors, especially short courses, have many of the advantages of books, including establishing an overall perspective. In addition, they tend to force one into action. It is easier to put off reading a book even after it is purchased than it is to put off a course once registered. Courses also provide a forum for discussion and personal interaction that serves an important function. Following is a list of some well-known companies that teach short courses in microprocessors.

Integrated Computer Systems, Inc.
4445 Overland Avenue
Culver City, CA 90230
(213) 559-9265

InfoScope Inc.
160 Tices Lane
East Brunswick, NJ 08816
(201) 238-2220

Wintek Corp.
902 North 9th Street
Lafayette, IN 47904
(317) 742-6802

American Institute for Professional Education
Carnegie Building, Hillcrest Road
Madison, NJ 07940
(201) 377-7400

The American Management Association
135 West 50th Street
New York, NY 10020
(212) 586-8100

Institute for Advanced Technology
6003 Executive Boulevard
Rockville, MD 20852
(301) 468-8576

Massachusetts Institute of Technology
Center for Advanced Engineering Study
77 Massachusetts Avenue, Room 9-234
Cambridge, MA 02139
(617) 253-7444

Pro-Log Corporation
2411 Garden Road
Monterrey, CA 93940
(404) 372-4593

The Institute of Electrical and Electronics Engineers
345 East 47 Street
New York, NY 10017
(212) 644-7860

12.4. VENDOR LITERATURE

It usually takes only a postcard or a telephone call to get on a microprocessor manufacturer's mailing list. This results in receiving product announcements, technical literature, and price information on a continuing basis. Although less beneficial than some other approaches, the ratio of information received to energy expended is impressive.

12.5. HARDWARE USAGE

Insight into information read or heard is usually solidified by actually using hardware in some way. One way is to use a development kit. Since these can be purchased for about $200, they appear to be a worthwhile investment.

APPENDIX A. Abbreviations

AC	accumulator
ALU	arithmetic logic unit
ASCII	American Standard Code for Information Interchange, an eight-digit code for a set of characters including the alphabet
A/D	analog-to-digital
BCD	binary-coded decimal
CAD	computer-aided design
CAM	content addressable memory
CCD	charge-coupled device
CML	current-mode logic
CMOS	complementary metal-oxide semiconductor
CODEC	coder/decoder
CPU	central processing unit
CRC	cyclic redundancy code
CROM	control read-only memory
CRT	cathode ray tube
D FF	delay flip flop
DIP	dual-in-line package
DMA	direct memory access
DMOS	depletion-mode double-diffused doping MOS
D/A	digital-to-analog
EAROM	electrically alterable read-only memory
EBCDIC	extended binary-coded decimal interchange code, an alphanumeric code
ECL	emitter-coupled logic
EEPROM	electrically erasable PROM
EFL	emitter function logic
EFT	electronic funds transfer
EPROM	erasable programmable read-only memory
FAMOS	floating-gate avalanche MOS
FET	field effect transistor
FIFO	first-in, first-out storage (queue)

FPLA	field-programmable logic array
HEX	hexadecimal code
HLL	high-level language
HMOS	scaled MOS process
IC	integrated circuit
ICE	in-circuit emulator
I²L	integrated injection logic
IR	instruction register
I/O	input/output
JK FF	JK flip flop
K	1024
LED	light-emitting diode
LIFO	last-in, first-out storage (stack)
LSB	least significant bit
LSI	large-scale integration
MAR	memory address register
MDR	memory data register
MDS	microprocessor development system
MNOS	metal-nitride-oxide semiconductor
MODEM	modulator/demodulator
MPU	microprocessor unit
MSB	most significant bit
MSI	medium-scale integration
MTBF	mean time before failure
NMOS	n-channel metal-oxide semiconductor
OEM	original equipment manufacturer
PC	program counter
PCB	printed circuit board
PLA	programmable logic array
PMOS	p-channel metal-oxide semiconductor
PROM	programmable read-only memory
PSW	processor status word
UART	universal asynchronous receiver/transmitter
USART	universal synchronous/asynchronous receiver/transmitter
USRT	universal synchronous receiver/transmitter
RALU	register arithmetic logic unit
RAM	random-access (read/write) memory
RMM	read-mostly memory
ROM	read-only memory
RS FF	set-reset flip flop
SBC	single-board computer
SOS	silicon on sapphire

SP	stack pointer
SSI	small-scale integration
T FF	trigger flip flop
TTL	transistor-transistor logic
TTY	teletype
VHSIC	very high speed integrated circuit
VLSI	very large scale integration
VMOS	V-geometry MOS
XOR	exclusive-OR
μ**C**	microcomputer
μ**P**	microprocessor

APPENDIX B. Glossary

Absolute Addressing   Specific permanently assigned address.

Access   Making electrical contact: for example, to read a word from memory.

Accumulator (AC)*   Register that contains results obtained from arithmetic, logical, shifting, and testing operations.

Accumulator Addressing   Addressing mode in which an operand is assumed to be present in the accumulator prior to the operation.

Acknowledge   Control signal to indicate acceptance of data in an I/O process.

Adder   Unit that does binary addition.

Address   Number associated with a particular memory location.

Algorithm   Programmable step-by-step procedure that converges to yield an answer to a problem.

Alphanumeric   Descriptor for alphabetic or numeric characters.

Analog   Represented by continuous information (e.g., voltage).

Analog-to-Digital (A/D)* Converters   Devices for converting an analog voltage input into an equivalent digital word output.

AND   Operation yielding logical "1" if and only if all inputs are 1.

Architecture   Basic system implementation or connection of standard modules.

Arithmetic logic unit (ALU)*   Circuitry for combining operands and operators to perform, for example, addition, subtraction, exclusive-ORing, shifting, and complementing.

Assembler   Program (resident in the computer) for converting assembly language to machine language.

Assembly Language   Representation of machine language that gives the

*Often expressed as an acronym.

programmer easier use by (1) representing instruction bit patterns by mnemonic codes and (2) representing memory locations by mnemonic codes.

Asynchronous Not tied to a common clock (operating outside the CPU clock constraints).

Batch Sequential processing of submitted programs.

Baud Symbols-per-second communication rate.

Benchmark Program Programmed solution to a standard task designed to assess the performance of various computers (or microcomputers) comparatively.

Bidirectional Data flows in either direction (as in bidirectional bus).

Bipolar Transistors Transistors that convey electrical energy by both electron motion and hole motion.

Bit-Slice Microprocessors Microprocessors that are intended to be concatenated or strung together to give almost arbitrary word size capability.

Bits Binary digits.

Boolean Operations Logical operations such as AND, OR, NOT, exclusive-OR.

Bootstrap Loader Loader that loads itself into memory after a key instruction or instructions (called a ''bootstrap'') has been inserted (or in read out of ROM).

Branch Change in the sequence of execution of the program instructions by jumping ahead or back (altering the program counter) in program memory.

Breadboard Prototype circuit intended to check out operation without regard to packaging.

Bubble Memory Memory utilizing microscopic magnetic domains in an aluminum–garnet substrate.

Buffer Register for temporary storage of data that can allow the data to be output at different times or rates from the input data.

Bugs Used to mean either (1) software errors causing unwanted behavior, (2) functional problems due to hardware errors, or (3) dual-in-line (DIP) packages.

Burn-in Operating a device at an elevated temperature to improve the probability that any device weakness will cause a failure.

Bus Group of lines for transmitting a group of associated bits for data transfer or control.

Byte Group (usually 8) of binary digits (bits).

Cache   High-speed memory used as a buffer between main memory and the CPU.

Call   Instruction that switches the PC to a subroutine address.

Cassette   Small cartridge containing ¼ in. magnetic tape used for micro-computer mass storage.

Cathode Ray Tube (CRT)*   Display device of the type used in television sets and oscilloscopes.

Central Processing Unit (CPU)*   Sequential logic circuit (typically a single chip) containing the arithmetic logic unit, the instruction decoding circuitry, timing and control circuits, temporary storage registers, and a program counter.

Chip   Small piece of semiconductor substrate (usually containing an integrated circuit).

Clock   Basic timekeeping mechanism, delivering periodic signals to which all activities are synchronized.

Code   According to context can be used as (1) a digital representation of numbers, letters, or symbols; (2) a program.

Codec   Coder/decoder for converting analog information (typically voice) to digital data, and for converting digital data to equivalent analog information.

Combinational Logic   Circuit for mapping digital inputs to a digital output or outputs. Combinational logic consists of gates and inverters and has no memory.

Compiler   Translation program for converting compiler language (source code) to machine language (object code).

Compiler Language   Higher-order language oriented toward making the programmer's job easier by approximating his common usage. FORTRAN, ALGOL, and BASIC are examples of compiler languages.

Complement   Changing 1's to 0's and 0's to 1's.

Computer   Relatively high speed device containing a CPU to execute instructions, memory, I/O, and software.

Core   Small magnetic toroid used in computer memories.

Cross Assembler   Program run on one computer to assemble (convert from assembly language to machine language) a program for another computer.

Cross Compiler   Program run on one computer to compile (convert from compiler language to an object code) program for another computer.

Cycle Stealing Use of part of an instruction cycle or cycles (when the buses are not being used by the CPU) to perform DMA.

Daisy Chaining Succession or chain of I/O ports connected by combinational logic so as to pass a signal along the chain until the first active source is detected and to block detection of subsequent active sources until the first active source has been acknowledged.

Data Terminal Device typically containing a teletype keyboard, telephone line modem, and cassette tape memory. A data terminal is used to communicate with computer time-share networks and processor-based systems.

Debouncing Hardware latch or software delay to allow switch contact bounce to cease (typically a few milliseconds).

Debugger Program with the capability to identify program locations for more detailed examination, for example, through single-step operation.

Decoder Combinational logic device which provides an output signal on one of 2^n possible output lines in response to the particular combination of input values on n input lines.

Delay (D) Flip Flop Shift register element whose output follows the input one clock time later.

Demultiplexer Circuit that electronically switches an input to one of several outputs.

Development System Development systems for particular microprocessors usually contain the microprocessor CPU, ROM, RAM, clock, and I/O. PROM chips can be inserted in order to test software by executing programs on the development system.

Die, Dice Sometimes used to describe chips (integrated circuit on a piece of semiconductor material).

Digital Representation by discrete levels, numbers, or digits.

Digital Data Data represented by digits in some number base system or code system.

Digital-to-analog (D/A)* Converters Devices for converting a digital word into an equivalent analog voltage output.

Direct Addressing Addressing mode where the required address is part of the instruction.

Direct Memory Access (DMA)* I/O transfer to or from a microprocessor-based system memory directly without CPU involvement.

Disk Magnetic recording device for mass storage using a flat, circular recording medium.

Diskette   Thin, circular flexible sheet of Mylar with a magnetic-oxide surface on which data can be recorded in tracks and from which data can be read. Sometimes called a floppy disk.

Duplex   Simultaneous bidirectional data transmission (by multiplexing or separate lines).

Dynamic RAM*   RAM that stores memory bits on capacitors, which must be periodically refreshed to prevent loss of data due to capacitive discharge.

EAROM*   Electrically alterable read-only memory. This can be written by inserting data in the form of trapped charge in memory cells. Selective rewriting can alter the memory. However, write times are sufficiently long that the devices cannot be considered to be RAMs.

Editor   Program that provides the capability to make changes, additions, and deletions to a program stored in a computer file without retyping the entire program.

Emulator   Hardware devices similar to development systems which allow programs to be run on actual hardware. They usually have such additional capabilities as program stops at specific locations and single-step operation. They are sometimes called in-circuit emulators, or ICEs.

Encoder   Converts input information to different output information, for example decimal switch positions to BCD code.

EPROM*   Erasable programmable read-only memory. The programming of the memory deposits trapped charge, which can be removed (for the entire device) by exposure to an intense source of ultraviolet light.

Error-Correcting Code   Technique of representing data by a pattern, including more bits than the minimum possible, with the extra (redundant) bits used to establish parity (or similar) equations whose solution allows errors to be detected or corrected.

Excess-3 Code   Coding scheme for decimal digits where 0 is coded as 0011 (binary representation of three), 1 is coded as 0100 (binary representation of four), and so on, through nine.

Exclusive-OR (XOR)*   Operation between two binary digits yielding a result of 1 if one and only one of the two digits has value 1, and yielding a result of 0 otherwise.

Execute Cycle   Processor operation during which a program instruction is carried out.

Fan-in   Number of outputs that can be accepted as inputs.

Fan-out   Number of inputs than can be driven by the output.

Fetch Cycle   A processor operation for reading an instruction from program memory into the CPU.

FIFO* A first-in, first-out memory consisting of a series of registers capable of containing words and connected so data are entered at one end (register) of the memory and are read out at the other end. FIFOs are sometimes called queues.

Firmware Software that has been made part of the hardware: for example by putting it in ROM.

Flag Indicator bit, typically stored in a flip flop.

Flip Flop Device that can temporarily store a binary digit (bit). Device input circuitry can include combinational logic.

Floppy Disk Low-cost mass storage medium usually consisting of a thin, circular flexible sheet of Mylar with a magnetic-oxide surface on which data can be recorded in tracks and from which data can be read. Sometimes called a *diskette.*

Flow Diagram Symbolic block diagram of program logic.

Gate Combinational logic device for providing an output signal in response to the intended combination of input signals. The gate has no memory.

Half-Duplex Information transmission limited to one direction at a time.

Hamming Code Single-error-correcting code.

Handshaking Two-way communication between an I/O device and the CPU to effect an I/O transfer.

Hardware Circuit components and associated equipment.

Hexadecimal Code Representation scheme for binary data where each group of 4 bits is represented by the hexadecimal (base 16) equivalent digit. The common convention for the 16 digits is 0 through 9 followed by A through F.

High-Level Language Powerful user-oriented language such as a compiler language or a highly capable interpreter.

Hollerith Code IBM punched-card code.

Immediate Addressing Instruction mode where the data to be used are part of the instruction.

In-Circuit Emulator (ICE)* Hardware device with a CPU, ROM, RAM, and I/O intended to run programs. The device usually has such additional capabilities as program stops at specific locations and single-step operation.

Index Register Register used to modify specified addresses in the indexed addressing mode.

Indexed Addressing Addressing mode where the contents of a specified index register are added to the specified address to obtain an effective address.

Indirect Addressing   Addressing mode where the address specified is the location where the address to be used can be found.

Input/Output (I/O)*   Interface between processor-based systems and the external word for communicating input or output data.

Instruction Cycle   CPU activity: carrying out an instruction, including fetch, decode, execute, and interrupt inquiry.

Instruction Register (IR)*   Storage register where an instruction from program memory is held for decoding.

Intelligent Terminals   Terminals that process data in a nontrivial way (editing, sorting, coding, etc.).

Interpretive Language   High-order language similar to compiler language, but each statement is converted to machine language individually.

Interrupt   I/O process initiated by an external signal requesting CPU access.

JK Flip Flop   Flip flop that can be "set" to 1 by the J input, "reset" to 0 by the K input, or "triggered" (from 0 to 1 or from 1 to 0) by simultaneous inputs.

Jump   Change in sequence of the execution of the program instructions, altering the program counter (i.e., a branch).

K   Symbol for 1,024.

Label   Symbolic address.

Language   Method for communicating with a processor by entering symbols (for example, numbers, alphabetic characters, mathematical operators) into the system. Variations range from machine-oriented languages (sequences of bit patterns) to people-oriented languages (words and equations).

Latch   Temporary storage device or register that retains input data until unlatched.

Library   Collection of software programs or routines.

LIFO*   Last-in, first-out memory consisting of a series of registers acting as a stack. A word read from a LIFO must be the last word written to the LIFO. LIFOs are sometimes called push-down stacks or push-pop stacks.

Light-Emitting Diode   Gallium arsenide, or similar, diodes that emit light when conducting current.

Linkage   Method of calling a subroutine and returning to the calling program.

Lithography   Process of masking surface for selective processing.

Loader   Software program for loading a program into memory.

Logic Analyzer   Device that allows CRT display of logic states in digital form or logic signals in analog form. Logic analyzers typically have multiple probes and multiple traces.

Loop   Sequence of instructions that is executed repeatedly until some test allows an escape to an instruction outside the loop.

Machine Language   Basic bit patterns a CPU is designed to interpret as instructions.

Macroinstruction   Machine language instruction, often representing several basic operations or microinstructions.

Macros   Assembler pseudo-instruction representing a subprogram or sequence of instructions defined by the programmer and reproduced in memory at each macro call.

Magnetic Cores   Small doughnut-shaped devices that retain permanent magnetic flux in one of two directions. These devices are often used in large-scale computer memory systems.

Memory   Locations for temporary or permanent storage of digital data.

Memory Address Register (MAR)*   Buffer register for temporarily storing addresses prior to putting them on the address bus.

Memory Data Register (MDR)*   Buffer register for temporarily storing data during transfer between the CPU and memory.

Memory-Mapped I/O   Addressing I/O devices in the same way that memory is addressed.

Microcomputer   Small, low-cost computer system based on a microprocessor CPU and including provisions for input (such as a keyboard, paper tape reader, etc.), output (such as a printer, numeric display, or CRT), and memory (ROM, RAM). The microcomputer system also includes a software operating system for program handling.

Microcontroller   According to context, used as (1) a microprocessor-based logic system dedicated to exercising some sort of system control, or (2) a microprogrammed control system.

Microinstruction   The constituent steps (usually hardwired into a processor) that must be taken to execute a machine language instruction. Microinstructions can be specified in microprogrammable microprocessors.

Microprocessor   Digital electronics-logic package, usually on a single chip, capable of performing the instruction execution, control, and data processing associated with a computer CPU. The device usually contains an arithmetic logic unit (ALU), temporary storage registers, instruction decode circuitry, timing and control circuitry, a program counter, and bus interface circuitry.

Microprocessor Analyzer   Similar to a logic analyzer (displays logic states in digital form or logic signals in analog form), but also oriented to micro-processor operation and control (can read and display data at or offset from specified memory or program addresses).

Microprogramming   Basic means of achieving desired instruction action by programming microinstructions for fundamental operations (e.g., register transfer, shift, add, decisions, and so on).

Mnemonic Codes   Symbolic names for instructions, registers, addresses, and so on.

Modem*   Modulator/demodulator. Device for modulating digital data onto a carrier signal (high frequency) and for demodulating the data off the carrier. The modulated carrier is effective for transmission over a telephone line, for example.

Monitor   Software-operating system that controls program flow so the user can enter programs, change programs, and so on.

Multiplexer   Circuit for electronically switching one of several inputs to an output.

Multiplexing   Electronically switching buses or groups of lines between a group of inputs or outputs.

Multiprocessing   Carrying on several processing operations simultane-ously.

N-Type Semiconductor   Semiconductor material doped with an impurity so that it conducts electrical energy by electron motion.

NAND   Logical operation yielding 0 if and only if all inputs are 1.

Nested Loops   Technique of programming loops within loops so that the inner loop is executed repeatedly until its escape condition is satisfied; each successive loop follows the same pattern until the escape condition for the outer loop is satisfied.

Nested Subroutines   Subroutine calls programmed within subroutines (*nesting*).

Nibble   Group of 4 binary digits (bits).

Nonvolatile Memory   Memory that is retained when power is shut off.

NOR   Logical operation yielding 1 if and only if all inputs are 0.

Object Code   Output of a software translation program like a compiler or assembler.

Op-Code (Operation Code)*   Part of an instruction that determines the next operation to be performed.

P-Type Semiconductor   Semiconductor material doped with an impurity so that it conducts electrical energy through the motion of voids (holes) in the crystalline structure.

Packing   Putting more than one word of information in a processor word.

Page   Segment of memory that can be specified by a subset (usually 8) of the bits in the complete address.

Page-Zero Addressing   Addressing mode where the most significant bits of the address (corresponding to a page address) are understood to be zero. Only the least significant bits of the address are specified.

Paged Direct Addressing   Addressing mode where the address is understood to be within a page section of memory. The least significant bits of the PC, which determine location within the page, are specified.

Parity   Result of an exclusive-OR check of the number of 1 bits in a word which gives odd parity if the number of 1's is odd and even parity if the number of 1's is even. Parity can be expressed by an additional bit (usually a 1 for odd parity and a 0 for even parity).

Personal Computers   Computers intended for use in the home by hobbyists or for operations not related to business.

Photolithography   Selective "masking" of a photosensitive emulsion-coated surface.

Pipelining   Processing strategy for getting data preprocessed or fetched in advance of their need so that wait time is minimized.

Pointer   Register containing an address of a memory location to be utilized.

Polling   Sequential examination of possible input or interrupt sources to look for one that is active.

Pop   Operation for reading a word out of stack memory.

Port   Device for I/O interfacing between a processor-based system and the external world.

Priority Interrupt   Technique for servicing interrupts on the basis of their assigned priority.

Processor   Device for interpreting and acting on program inputs.

Program Counter (PC)*   Register containing the address of the next instruction to be executed. At turn-on or reset time, the program counter is normally set to 0. After each instruction is executed, the program counter advances one count unless changed by program control.

Programmable Logic Array   MSI or LSI device capable of realizing several functions of several input variables.

Programming   According to context, can be used in various ways, including (1) writing a sequence of instructions, (2) physically inserting data into

ROM or PROM, or (3) setting up an address by electrical connections to which particular devices (memory elements or input/output devices) will respond.

PROM* User-programmable read-only memory, in which data can be permanently fixed by the user by using a PROM programmer.

PROM Programmer Device that can be used to insert data into a PROM.

Pseudo-Instruction Assembly language instruction, not directly related to a machine language instruction, but used by the assembler to take some action affecting the generation of the machine language program.

Pseudo-Random Sequence Sequence whose properties closely approximate testable randomness properties, although the sequence is completely deterministic.

Push Operation for putting a word into stack memory.

Push-Down Stack Last-in, first-out memory (LIFO) stack consisting of registers for temporary storage of words, for example, during subroutine execution.

Queue First-in, first-out memory (FIFO)

RAM* Random-access memory, more descriptively called a read/write memory since data can be written into it as well as read out from it.

Random Access Memory access to a specified location without waiting to arrive at the data or data location sequentially.

Read Process of examining data in memory by deriving signals that directly represent the data. Reading is usually a nondestructive process. That is, the data are unaltered in memory after the read process.

Refresh Replenish the discharge from the memory capacitors (recharging) in a dynamic RAM.

Register Storage device for temporarily storing a group of associated bits.

Register-Arithmetic Logic Unit (RALU)* Bit-slice device consisting of an ALU and associated registers that can be concatenated to form a bit-slice processor.

Register Direct Addressing Addressing mode where the operand or data destination is contained in a register specified in the Op-code.

Register Indirect Addressing Addressing mode where the register specified by the Op-code contains the address to be used.

Relative Addressing Addressing mode where an offset is specified for addition to or subtraction from the PC.

Resident Assembler Program for converting assembly language programs to machine language programs such that the assembler is stored within the processor system on which it is to be run.

Resident Compiler   Program for converting compiler language programs to machine language programs such that the compiler is stored within the processor system on which it is to be run.

ROM*   Read-only memory from which data can be obtained and in which the data are permanently fixed according to specification when ordering the part.

Scratch Pad Memory   CPU registers used for writing and reading data.

Semiconductor   Material having intermediate resistivity (neither a conductor nor an insulator).

Sequential Logic   Circuit including combinational logic and memory so that the output or outputs are a function of the inputs and memory.

Set-Reset Flip Flop   Flip flop that can be ''set'' to 1 or ''reset'' to 0.

Simulator   Program that allows simulated execution of a program by running it on another machine. A simulator might be used, for example, to execute a microprocessor program on a large-scale computer.

Software   Programs of instructions, including the operating programs and programs for editing, program conversion, and loading data into memory.

Source Code   Input to a software translation program that yields object code.

Stack   Series of registers or memory locations for storing needed data during periods of departure from the main program (interrupts and subroutines).

Stack Addressing   Addressing mode where the address to be used is contained in a *stack pointer register*.

Stack Pointer   Register that contains an address that identifies an area in memory called a *stack* for storing needed data during periods of departure from the main program (*interrupts and subroutines*).

Static RAM   RAM that retains memory without refreshing until the memory is rewritten or until power is removed.

Status Register   Register indicating the results of the last accumulator operation, such as positive or negative, zero, odd or even parity, carry.

Subroutine   Subprogram (set of self-contained instructions) that can be called for execution whenever the programmer desires by changing the PC. At the end of the subroutine execution, the PC is changed back to the calling program.

Subroutine Call   Main program instruction for changing the PC to the subroutine location. This instruction typically provides automatic storage of the return address in the calling routine on a stack.

Subroutine Return   Instruction for changing the PC back to the main program. The return address is typically obtained automatically from a stack.

Synchronous   System operation keyed to a common time source (clock).

Teletype (TTY)*   Has a keyboard, printer, and a modem for communicating over a telephone line with a computer.

Trigger Flip Flop   Flip flop that changes state (1 to 0 or 0 to 1) in response to an input transition.

Tristate Bus Driver   Device for transmitting data onto a bus that can drive the bus either to a voltage representing a logic 1; to a voltage representing a logic 0; or can assume a high-impedance state so that the bus can be controlled by other devices.

Truth Table   Table listing outputs as a function of all possible input combinations.

Universal Asynchronous Receiver/Transmitter (UART)*   Interface device for serial/parallel conversion, buffering, and adding check bits.

Vectored Interrupt   Interrupt structure in which the first interrupt source to become active takes control of the data bus for part of the interrupt cycle in order to identify itself to the CPU.

Virtual Memory   Technique for addressing mass memory peripherals (disk, drum, tape) utilizing special software for transferring to and from fast-access memory.

Volatile Memory   Memory that is lost when power is removed.

Wafer   Thin slice of silicon or other semiconductor substrate material, usually about 2 to 3 in. in diameter.

Word   Group of associated digits.

Write   Process of inserting data into memory. This is a destructive process, in that any data already in a particular memory location are destroyed when new data are written into that location.

APPENDIX C. Numerology

1802	RCA "Cosmac" 8-bit microprocessor.
2708	One of the most popular EPROMs, a 1,024 × 8 ultraviolet-erasable ROM.
2716	Intel EPROM; 2,048 × 8 organization.
2901	Popular bit-slice processor.
2920	Analog processor.
3850	Fairchild F8 8-bit microprocessor CPU.
3851	Fairchild F8 program storage unit PSU, including a ROM, PC and other logic, and registers for working with the 3850.
4000	Standard product line of CMOS SSI and MSI logic circuits.
4004	First microprocessor, a 4-bit CPU developed by Intel Corporation.
6800	Popular 8-bit microprocessor made by Motorola.
8008	First general-purpose 8-bit microprocessor (Intel Corporation).
8080A	Improved version of the Intel 8008 8-bit microprocessor. The most popular microprocessor to date (basic version made by Intel Corporation).
8085	Improved version of 8080A.
8086	Intel 16-bit microprocessor.
8748	Intel single-chip "microcomputer."
68000	Motorola 16-bit microprocessor.
F8	Fairchild 3850 8-bit microprocessor CPU.
IEEE-488	Standard laboratory equipment system bus configuration.
RS232C	Computer/modem interface connection.
S100	Intel/Zilog system bus configuration.
TMS 1000	Texas Instruments 4-bit microprocessor with on-chip ROM, RAM.
Z8000	Zilog 16-bit microprocessor.

APPENDIX D. Hexadecimal Coding

Bit pattern	Hexadecimal symbol
0000	0
0001	1
0010	2
0011	3
0100	4
0101	5
0110	6
0111	7
1000	8
1001	9
1010	A
1011	B
1100	C
1101	D
1110	E
1111	F

Index

155